Nicole Weber

EQUIHYPNOSIS

Essential Techniques for Managing Riding Fear

FOUR
IN HAND

PRESS

AN IMPRINT OF TRAFALGAR SQUARE BOOKS

First published in 2025
by Four-In-Hand Press
an imprint of Trafalgar Square Books
The Stable Book Group
Brooklyn, New York

Originally published in German as *Equihypnose®—Wege aus der Angst beim Reiten*.

Disclaimer of Liability
The author and publisher shall have neither liability nor responsibility to any person or entity with respect to any loss or damage caused or alleged to be caused directly or indirectly by the information contained in this book. While the book is as accurate as the author can make it, there may be errors, omissions, and inaccuracies.

Trafalgar Square Books encourages the use of approved safety helmets in all equestrian sports and activities.

Trafalgar Square Books certifies that the content in this book was generated by a human expert on the subject, and the content was edited, fact-checked, and proofread by human publishing specialists with a lifetime of equestrian knowledge. TSB does not publish books generated by artificial intelligence (AI).

ISBN: 978-1-64601-299-2
Library of Congress Control Number: 2024923336

Photo credits: © Horseman / Fotolia.com: p. 19; © Taylon / Fotolia.com: p. 24; © Powell83 / Fotolia.com: p. 83; © Skumer / Fotolia.com: p. 30, 31; © Roman Bodnarchuk / Fotolia.com: p. 32; © Tatomm / Fotolia.com: p. 35; © Nadine Haase / Fotolia.com: p. 37; © Maytii / Fotolia.com: p. 41; MEV-Verlag: p. 89, 96, 103, 107; Anke Paulmann: p. 3, 20; Stefan Julius Römer: p. 140; Michelle Schlicker: pp. 4, 16, 43, 50, 51, 61, 62, 63, 66, 67, 68, 70, 72, 73, 74, 75, 84, 88, 90, 91, 100, 105, 109, 110, 112, 114, 115, 116, 117, 118, 120, 122, 124, 125, 126, 128, 136; Rebecca Spöring: pp. 8, 10, 13, 14, 45, 56, 57, 60, 134, 138; Weber Archive: p. 21, 40, 44, 49, 52, 53, 55, 58, 79, 80, 81, 87, 98, 142; Maren Weber: p. 38, 39, 54, 78, 141; Bea Wild: p. 9; front cover: Rebecca Spöring; back cover: Michelle Schlicker (top), Rebecca Spöring (bottom)

German editor: Claudia König
Translation into English: Nicole Weber
English editor: Kamille Parkinson
Cover design: RM Didier
Interior design: Kornelia Erlewein

Printed in China
10 9 8 7 6 5 4 3 2 1

Important Note

Never ride without a helmet.
In some older pictures in this book,
you will see a rider who is not wearing
a riding helmet, but this is an outdated
practice. For their own safety, all riders
should wear properly fitted riding
helmets. Wearing a riding helmet is
expressly recommended by
the author and publisher.

SONNENREITER

Table of Contents

Part 2

Foreword
by Jenny Wild & Peer Classen

Nicole Weber

We met Nicole Weber at a large equine trade show in Hannover, Germany. From the very first contact, it became clear how well we were on the same wavelength—even though we work in very different fields. The common denominator is our daily commitment to making the relationship between horse and human safer and more harmonious.

Horses, being flight animals, are very easily unsettled, and their flight responses can frighten us humans. This leads to a multitude of insecurities and defensive behaviors on both sides, which must be resolved to transform opposition into cooperation.

Our focus is on behavior. At the heart of our work with horses and people are the two concepts: focus and energy. Focus is our concentration, our inner and outer gaze, our clarity. Energy determines how that focus feels for us and for the horse: strong or weak, abundant or scarce, deliberate or scattered, etc. However, the most important area is unfortunately also the one we find hardest to convey and influence: emotional energy. We can certainly explain and describe it through images and examples, and even demonstrate what we mean—and that often works. But we do not have direct access to the inner processes of our students, nor even our own. Insecurities and frustration, as well as joy and equanimity, come and go seemingly at will.

And this is exactly where Nicole Weber's approach comes in. She has that immediate access; she finds the direct path to the control centers of the unconscious and subconscious. Her methods restore the flow of positive energies and unlock potential. We, too, have experienced her abilities firsthand. Without any unnecessary frills, she simply, honestly, and authentically offers help exactly where it is needed. We were impressed, on the one hand, by the openness with which she explains causes and effects, and on the other hand by the complete package in which the horse and the interaction with him play a decisive role. True help can only be achieved when all factors of an equation are considered, and in this case, understanding the horse cannot be neglected. Horse and rider continuously influence each other. To work together in an atmosphere free of fear and full of openness, one

Jenny & Peer

must understand how and why horses are mentally and emotionally influenced by us. For only then can a true partnership develop.

Every horse has its own personality, yet they are also highly sensitive to even the slightest changes in their counterpart, whether that is a predator, another horse, or a human. It is essentially our duty to care for inner strength, power, and security if we want to do justice to the horses. For a horse, it is most important to have an effective, strong, and reliable partner by his side. Once it has that, he will readily offer his abilities in return.

Unfortunately, traditional training methods often originate in insecurities. After all, what else are crop chains, harsh bits, and heavy-handedness good for? But it's not just a controlling behavior driven by a fear for one's life and limb; the need for recognition, exam stress, and performance pressure are ultimately just different forms of various fears. They all tempt us to work against the horse rather than with him.

Nicole Weber offers you a guide to self-help. She shows you ways to break free from the spiral of fear. The book is, therefore, an encouragement—not only in a figurative sense. With the self-hypnosis exercises, you can leave behind various insecurities for the sake of mutual success. In doing so, you will become exactly the partner your horse desires. In truth, these exercises offer you a much greater service than you might believe and will have a lasting impact.

Yours,

Jenny and Peer

Introduction

*F*ear is a feeling everyone has experienced. It is a response that is necessary for our survival. But fear also has the potential to plunge us into deep suffering if it prevents us from doing what brings us joy. I have written this book to help you transition away from fear, and journey back to a place that brings you happiness.

At some point, almost every rider has felt fear while interacting with her horse. This is a normal reaction to a frightening situation, and as long as the fear subsides, it isn't an issue. However, when fear starts to accompany us while riding, when our interactions with our horse are dominated by fear, we need to make a change. Unfortunately, it's at times like this that a well-intentioned person may tell a fearful rider something along the lines of: "You have to ride through your fear," or, "Don't let your horse feel that you are afraid," as if fear is something inside us we can easily or successfully mask. Those people are trying to be helpful, but if we aren't able to "ride through it" as they suggest, we may feel even worse. In addition, the horse cannot actually be deceived by our attempts to hide our feelings. Horses are invaluable for psychotherapeutic work because they are emotional seismographs. They perceive even the feelings we hide from ourselves, and that is why they will always react to our fears, sometimes with what we perceive as unhelpful behaviors.

But if that's the case—if the fear simply doesn't want to go away, and you don't want to give up your relationship with horses—what should you do? Well, as always, the first step is to admit that you have a problem. You have already successfully done that; otherwise, you would not be holding this book in your hands. The purpose of this book is to show you ways to free yourself from your fear.

Since fear is a feeling you can't control consciously (otherwise, you would have already done so), it is important to convince your subconscious that your fear is unnecessary. By doing so, you learn to feel safe in situations that do not threaten your physical or psychological well-being. This doesn't mean you will never feel fear again, because in situations that are actually dangerous, you should still feel fear. Rather, the aim of this book is to give you the tools to successfully manage fear that is impacting the pleasure you get from your horse and riding, with the goal of enabling you to enjoy your hobby and your partnership with your horse again. If you change, your horse will also change. Herein lies both the cause of and the solution to many problems with our equine partner. With the help of the exercises, videos, and MP3s provided in this book, you will change, and this will also change your horse's behavior.

And so, dear reader, I wish you all the best on your journey to free yourself from fear, and I thank you for allowing me to accompany you along the way through this book and its supplementary material. I wish you a lot of fun reading, and successful progress! Most of all, I wish you a (renewed) harmonious partnership with your horse.

Nicole Weber

How to Use This Book

I would like to explain just a few things before you start reading and working with this book. Principally, it's important that I establish a personal connection with you so that you as a conscious person feel addressed, and to help your subconscious mind accept the connection. This process is all about you—what you wish for and what you want to change. I have paid close attention to how I write everything, because even by just reading this text, you might start to experience those changes. Because I make sure that your subconscious mind also feels addressed by what I say, everything I have written here can have a hypnotic effect if you want it to.

You have already begun to change. You probably bought this book because you are tired of engaging in your hobby, your passion, without joy. You want a change for the better. You are ready for this change, you have put money into it (admittedly not as much as an in-person session with me would cost), and you are ready to do everything I recommend in the following pages. This means you have set a goal for yourself, and have already started making changes in your life. But you also know that only you can ensure that this change continues—with a little outside help. Together, we will explore your fear, and I will show you what you can do for yourself. Every day, in every way, you will feel better and better.

The first part of this book covers the theory around chronic fear and how it takes hold of us. It's important for you to read this part because I would like to explain to you how fears arise, what causes them, and why your horse mirrors your fear. You need to have that information for the later exercises to make sense. I will also address a few things beyond what I describe above.

The second part of the book is more hands-on and requires you to take action. In this part, you will learn what to do to leave your fears behind. To achieve this, I have provided you with everything you need to know, and with everything else you need to support you as you free yourself from fear. In addition to capturing in photographs how the exercises should look, I have also provided links to videos so you can see exactly how to replicate something. Essentially, you will learn self-hypnosis. I have recorded the instructions for you, and, in addition, you will find hypnosis MP3s that will support you on your journey. Not only will you be able to hypnotize yourself, but, using the MP3s, you may also choose to be hypnotized by me if you wish. Any fears you might have about hypnosis are also addressed in the second part of the book. If you are unsure whether hypnosis will be useful for you because you suffer from a chronic disease like epilepsy, or you have had a psychotic episode before, please consult your primary care physician.

If at any point while reading, you feel your fears may have a physical cause (such as a hormonal imbalance, food intolerance, or other chronic condition) please also consult a doctor. Additionally, if you become aware that the causes of your fear are very complex, or too heavy for you to bear on your own, please seek medical or psycho-therapeutic help.

No rider is perfect....

We all wish for a harmonious partnership.

The self-hypnosis MP3s are audio tracks that are either guided versions of the exercises, or a hypnosis audio, meant to help you move past fear. I will explain how to use them later in the book. With the help of the self-hypnosis MP3s, positive change can be even more profound, because you can let yourself sink deeper into a state of trance. It is usually not enough to just listen to them, however. You should perform self-hypnosis and do the other exercises as well, so you can reach your goal as quickly as possible and experience sustainable changes. I have structured this book in such a way that everything interconnects, for the greatest benefit to you. As an added bonus, this book and its exercises may also be used to alleviate chronic fears other than those related to riding.

It really does not matter if you perceive your riding fears to be great or small. This book is for you if you are afraid of trail riding or jumping. It is for you if fear has kept you from cantering or trotting. This book is also for you if it has been a long time since you've even thought about mounting your horse, or if you find yourself afraid of simply walking with your horse or otherwise interacting with him. You can overcome fears of all sizes. All of the exercises and self-hypnosis techniques can be implemented while riding or while working with your horse on the ground.

I also wrote this book for you if you are a trainer and want to better help your students. Please note, however, that in the following chapters I mainly address those who are themselves struggling with fear. If you are reading as an instructor, you will be able to pick out some things that may help you support your students, but do not attempt to hypnotize others. In particular, hypnotizing others to combat their fear belongs in experienced hands only. If, while reading this book, you find that hypnosis interests you, feel free to contact me. I regularly train hypnotists and hypnotherapists.

As you are reading and doing the exercises, you may notice that I make the same connections again and again. I do this because it helps them settle into your mind better. So if you realize that you have already read something specific, be happy: that means it has stuck. With each repetition, any given connection becomes more firmly embedded in your consciousness. As you go through this book, it is also a good idea to have a notebook of some kind handy, so you can write down things you find important for yourself. You will need this notebook for some of the exercises, too.

Before we get started on your journey to free yourself from fear, I wish to remind you of certain things, many of which you already know to be true. You have learned, during your life, to react with fear in certain situations, and in most cases, the fear you felt was productive (in its way) and manageable. In some cases, however, a learned fear can become unmanageable and paralyzing. Fortunately, we can unlearn things that do not serve us well. You can overcome your fear—don't let anyone tell you that you can't! It will take effort to overcome your fear (I would never suggest that reading this book will make your fear disappear as if by magic), but you don't have to worry that it will take years. In most cases, we are talking about just weeks or even days until you feel a significant improvement. Trust that you have the power and the ability to leave your fear behind.

You are now ready to start on your way to a new feeling of confidence and liberation from fear, no matter how long your fear has existed or how old you are. Everything you need to accomplish this is found in the following chapters, and though I have compiled it for you, it's up to you to make the change in yourself. So get started, and allow me to guide and accompany you into your inner world, where it is just about you and this problem we will overcome. Within yourself, you will discover the means to free yourself from fear and find your way back to the joy of riding.

Part 1

"Nothing in life is to be feared, it is only to be understood. Now is the time to understand more, so that we may fear less."

Marie Curie

Chapter 1: Development and Causes of Riding Fear

*D*o you sometimes wonder how you got to a point where you are afraid of riding, or even afraid of being around your horse? It's not a comfortable feeling, but you should know that you are not alone. Many riders, even professionals, have felt fear at some point in their lives while riding or interacting with horses. Maybe you know other riders who have managed to overcome these fears. Trust me when I tell you that you can do it, too!

Perhaps you have heard that you should ride through your fear. Maybe you have also heard that you should not let your horse feel your fear. You have probably tried both, and neither worked for you. As far as not letting your horse feel your fear is concerned, the issue with that so-called solution is straightforward—you cannot lie to horses. Horses are emotional seismographs and will pick up on emotions we think we have buried. However, the first piece of advice, riding through the fear, can actually work. If you know how.

The truth is that those who give this advice usually have no idea how to leave fear behind—both because they have not experienced your type of fear, and, importantly, because they are not trained in psychotherapy. When you hear that you should just ride through it, with the advice to, "Just canter already, you will see that you won't fall," it probably won't make you approach the next canter with more courage. Instead, you are more likely to ask yourself whether you are even a good rider.

This kind of well-meaning advice can unfortunately cause even more fear, if it comes from someone who doesn't really know what they are talking about. A recent client told me that a former trainer forced her to go on a two-hour trail ride, telling her, "After that, you'll know you don't need to be afraid." In behavioral therapy, this approach can indeed be used. However, in order for it to work, these kinds of confrontations with the fear-inducing moment or activity are mindfully set up by the behavioral therapist, who usually accompanies their client through that controlled scenario. This careful preparation means the most important result is achieved: no further terrible things happen.

Unfortunately, in this case, during this ride my client was forced to take, her horse was frightened and bolted. The trainer had no influence over the frightened horse, and ultimately my client fell off the bolting animal. Since that time, my client had not even mounted her horse again. She said that this ride had retraumatized her, and that she had lost all trust in her trainer. I can certainly understand.

I believe that if you want to help people with problems like this, you should at least have a basic knowledge of

No one is immune to falls, and no one is immune to fear.

psychology. You should also know how to solve these problems, and you should have successfully done so many times before. In my opinion, it is irresponsible for riding instructors to use their students as guinea pigs, as in the case described above, as it can have detrimental consequences.

Riders who have never been afraid of riding sometimes think fear is related to a lack of skill, and I have often heard fearful riders being told this is why they are afraid. However, fear has nothing to do with level of skill.

Nobody is immune to fear. Whether you get back on the horse after a fall does not depend on your degree of riding ability. It depends on how you process this fall, and on what kind of foundation this experience rests. If you're a mother, for example, you probably have your children in the back of your mind, and you know you need to stay safe so you can take care of them. Nature has cleverly arranged it so you will be more cautious as a result.

Even top professional riders who compete internationally can develop chronic fear. It's probably not something you've heard about, but believe me, it's not because it doesn't happen. There are a number of reasons why chronic fear within the ranks of professional riders isn't widely discussed. These may include: the person is reluctant to admit they are afraid because they are in the spotlight and are a sports role model; high-profile people are often quickly and unjustly criticized; less successful riders might take advantage of a well-known rider's fear to raise their own position and self-esteem. Given these reasons (among others), it's easy to understand why big-name trainers or professional riders don't reveal that they've experienced riding-related fear, or that they have sought help because they couldn't free themselves from that fear on their own. It could definitely tarnish their image.

I have worked with many professional riders and trainers, but they don't advertise this fact. Instead, this clientele shares my name discreetly amongst themselves, letting each other know I can help. So, while it is not advertised by professional equestrians, I think it is essential for you to know that you are not alone in your fear. On the contrary, you are in the good company of fantastic, talented, sensitive riders, and empathetic trainers. What connects you with these horse people who faced their fear are exactly these qualities, which I know you have, too.

It is because you are sensitive and empathetic that you developed chronic fear; and it is because you are sensitive and empathetic that you have the ability to become a wonderful partner to your horse again.

As I alluded to above, people who experience chronic fear are often ridiculed by those without fear. In my eyes, this reveals a lack of sensitivity and empathy. I frequently observe that when I announce a workshop on social media, for example, there are always negative comments, and people who try to make themselves look better than others. In my opinion, this behavior just shows how little these people know about the subject of fear and how to overcome it. But it's also because of the way many riding schools still teach today. Many riding instructors simply don't know how to deal with students who are afraid—after all, it wasn't part of the *trainer's* training.

A rearing horse doesn't necessarily have to scare his rider, as this rider's smile clearly shows.

It is not just horses that want to flee from some of the things encountered in the wild.

Ultimately, it doesn't matter why you have developed a riding-related fear. Maybe you were once a very brave rider and rode the wildest horses, and now you can't understand what has changed. Or perhaps you have always felt somewhat anxious, and have never seen yourself as a courageous rider. Whatever the case, it's crucial to understand that being anxious isn't innate, it's learned, and it often stems from a fear of losing control. Working with a horse accentuates this feeling, because we're partnering with a large, powerful creature with natural flight instincts that may act on his own feelings and judgments. This dynamic can make these situations especially challenging, compared to other contexts where chronic fears occur. Yet it's possible to learn to remain calm and poised in this kind of tense scenario, which can positively influence both the situation and the horse.

What Fear Wants to Tell You

At its core, fear has two components. The first is the cause, which has given rise to the fear, and the second is the *maintenance* of that fear. Let's look at both.

You may be familiar with this scenario: You're thinking about going to the barn later. Your horse really should be ridden again, though you've been avoiding that lately. You look out the window and realize it's windy. The thought crosses your mind that your horse is more prone to spooking in the wind. You recall that recently, on another windy day, a blanket flew off the fence. You were passing by the arena door at that moment, and saw a horse in the arena jump to the side because of the blowing blanket. The rider stayed on and briefly scolded her horse, and you were relieved that it wasn't you and your horse involved. Currently, you prefer riding in the arena, out of the elements, rather than the outdoor riding area. But now you're wondering if it might be better to skip riding entirely today, especially since thinking about it is making you feel so uneasy.

What this scenario shows is that you have a fear of fear itself, and your thoughts have only increased your fears and worries. When we ponder these kinds of things, we quickly fall into a kind of fear spiral, and these spiraling thoughts sustain our fears. By doing this, we basically train our fear, making it more readily available and more pronounced—the exact opposite of what we want.

This whirlwind of thoughts, in which we vividly imagine what could potentially happen, is essentially a form of negative self-hypnosis. When we visualize something with great clarity and intensity, we enter a type of trance. In this state, we're especially receptive, our brains are at their most malleable, and we learn more quickly. That's usually a good thing—but not when it comes to fear.

I want you to know that, because of your vivid imagination and sensitivity, you easily enter into a trance and are also highly suggestible. Together, this strong suggestibility and easy ability to enter a trance is both a blessing and a curse. I've already explained the way in which these characteristics are a curse: With your imagination and the power of your visualizations about your fear, you ensure that you can feel fear more quickly and intensely. It's like negative self-hypnosis, by which you train yourself to get better at becoming afraid. The blessing is that your suggestibility also makes it easy for you to leave your fears behind, through the same process. You just have to find a way to use your powers of imagination to your advantage. I'll show you how in the next chapters. Moreover, afterward you'll be able to harness this powerful imaginative ability for all other goals in your life.

Physical Symptoms

Fear is an emotion designed to ensure our survival. Physically, fear mobilizes all our energy reserves to activate the "fight or flight" response, as our systems flood with stress hormones such as adrenaline, norepinephrine, and cortisol, which keep us alert and attentive. These hormones also ensure we don't immediately perceive pain if something harms us. Our breathing rate accelerates to provide our muscles with more oxygen. Our heart rate significantly increases so more blood can be pumped to the large muscle groups and internal organs; to allow for this increased blood flow, the blood vessels in our legs expand, which is why you might feel like you have shaky legs. The overall increase in muscle tension can make your hands tremble, too.

There's often a queasy feeling in our midsections, pressure in our chests, sweating, and altered skin coloration. In addition to all that, we might feel dizzy, hear ringing in our ears, or urgently need to use the restroom.

The physical symptoms of fear are diverse, and may or may not include those described above. Moreover, they don't all necessarily occur simultaneously, and you might experience symptoms other than the ones I've listed. Each person is unique, and will respond to fear in slightly different ways.

HOW DOES YOUR FEAR MANIFEST?

What are the three or four main symptoms you experience when you feel fear? Please write them down. For each symptom, think about where you would rate it on a scale from 1-10 (1 = the symptom is very mild, 10 = it couldn't be more intense). Also, assign an overall value to your riding fear on this scale.

Keep this note handy, as you'll need it later to assess how your fear has changed.

Emotional And Behavioral Symptoms

Besides the physical symptoms, fear also induces changes in our emotional state and behavior. We become easily irritable and tense, because fear causes stress, especially if it has become chronic, and stress produces these behaviors. When we are in a state of fear, our ability to focus is impaired significantly, and we do not act rationally. For instance, every rider knows they shouldn't shout while riding. If you are intensely afraid, however, this knowledge is forgotten, and you might scream, even though under other circumstances you are aware it might worsen the situation. Over time, fear develops into a spiral of anxiety during which we constantly think about what triggers our fear.

Because this kind of thought spiral can make it difficult to sleep, chronic fear can also affect our rest. You might lie awake longer, wake up in the middle of the night and feel unable to fall back asleep, or find yourself waking up very early in the morning. Your thoughts may go in circles, and you might almost feel as if you're going mad. None of this seems normal to you, but you try to cope on your own because you wonder what others would think of you if you told them how you are feeling.

Gradually, you start avoiding what scares you. You might have firmly decided to go trail riding today to prove to yourself that you still can. You're not exactly comfortable with the thought, however, so you decide that a brief ride around the property at a walk will suffice. As you leave the house, however, you notice that it's drizzling. During the drive to the stable, you wonder whether the drizzle will intensify and turn to rain. You don't like rain, but worse, rain makes your horse jittery. Lately, too, you tell yourself, your horse has started to object to even the sound of rain on the arena roof. You decide you should postpone the ride outside for a nicer day. So, upon arriving at the stable, you take the cavesson, lunge line, and whip from the tack locker, instead of your saddle. Better safe than sorry, you tell yourself.

The added difficulty with any fear is that it becomes chronic if it isn't addressed promptly. The longer a fear persists, the less likely it is to resolve on its own, and instead it may require treatment. Fear may also spread to different areas of your life. Many of my patients have gone through an "anxiety career," starting, for instance, with a fear of heights, and then gradually accumulating other fears—related fears, at first, and then unrelated fears. If you suffer from multiple phobias, you might have experience with this. Fear sends us into a spiral of anxiety. We eventually fear the onset of fear itself, which only amplifies our anxiety.

Most riders who develop chronic fear believe they can pinpoint the exact cause of their anxiety.

Falling Is Not the Cause of Your Fear

Diana reports: "Three years ago, I had a nasty fall during a trail ride. I was out riding with a friend when our horses got spooked by a combine harvester and bolted. After some time, we managed to slow the horses down, but then a tractor approached us. I thought my horse would bolt again, so I tried to hold him back. That's when he lowered his head and began to buck. He had never behaved like that before, which caught me off guard. At first, I could manage the bucks, but then my horse really started acting like a rodeo bronco. At least that's what my friend says—I can't recall the details. At some point, I know, I just couldn't hold on anymore, and I fell off. After a hospital stay, rehabilitation, and several months of recovery, I was allowed to ride again."

Diana goes on to say, "Since the fall, I've been afraid of going on trail rides. Over the past few months, even cantering in an arena has become difficult. The thing is, I have two horses—the gelding I fell from, and a mare—and strangely, I am much more afraid of the mare than of the gelding, even though nothing bad ever happened with her."

In this example with Diana, you might assume that the fall led directly to her fear. But if that was the case, why would she feel more fear of the mare, with whom she never had a traumatic experience, than the gelding from whom she had actually fallen? Something doesn't add up, and that demonstrates that there are other factors influencing her reaction.

It could be that, due to other experiences or beliefs about her abilities or about the nature of horses in general, Diana became insecure. Maybe she picked up somewhere, or developed the conviction herself, that mares are more temperamental than geldings. Or perhaps, early on, the mare exhibited behavior that Diana interpreted as unpredictable, even if it wasn't dangerous at the time, and now she subconsciously remembers that, and the context of her new fear makes it much more frightening. Fear is not always logical. It's entirely possible that Diana's fear, through a combination of physical memories of the fall and psychological factors, was transferred from the gelding to the mare.

We tend to want to make causal connections between certain events and our reactions to them. In doing so, we often forget that our feelings, reactions, and beliefs are the result of a multitude of influences—not just a single experience. So it is essential to recognize that while traumatic events like falling off a horse and becoming severely injured can definitely lead to fear, they often serve as *triggers,* while the underlying *causes* are usually much deeper and more complex, and very often have nothing to do with horses whatsoever.

Conclusion: A fall can be a trigger that "sets off" fear, but in most cases, it's not the root cause.

THE FUNCTION OF FEAR

Fear is fundamentally a very meaningful and necessary response to danger. We are born with the ability to feel fear, and every animal and human is hardwired to experience it. We need this ability, because fear activates the alarm system of our bodies when we are in danger. Only when it is triggered are we able to flee, fight, or freeze. Fear is meant to ensure our survival, so we need it to respond appropriately and swiftly in dangerous situations. Fear is not something you should despise. In genuinely dangerous situations, fear is your ally.

It can happen, however, that fear becomes misplaced, and we start to feel fear in situations that are not actually dangerous. The body's alarm system doesn't always respond correctly. Maybe we fear something in the future, or even the past. Maybe we start to fear everyday activities that most people find unproblematic. There's also a heightened sense of fear that can escalate to *panic,* which can strike seemingly without warning. Panic manifests mainly physically, and it can make us feel as if we are dying.

A life full of fear is not desirable, but neither is a life without fear. You should feel fear in dangerous situations, in order to keep yourself safe. On the other hand, when no part of you is actually at risk, you should not feel unwarranted fear. Paradoxically, we live in a society where fear is part of everyday life, especially because most of us live in safe places. Sociologists call it the "security paradox." Because we have security, we subconsciously fear losing it, which is why, in the countries that are safest to live in worldwide, people tend to be particularly fearful. This doesn't mean you can't do anything about your fears.

HOW CHRONIC FEAR DEVELOPS

Fear can arise in different ways. In this section, we will explore some of them.

Fear can be transferred.

"Transferred fear" means you have learned to react to certain things with fear because you picked up on the fear triggers of those around you. For example, if certain fears are demonstrated by parents or grandparents, children quickly pick up on this behavior. It doesn't even have to be the same fear or phobia. Often, children just learn that fear is an adequate response to different things. As a result, it's not uncommon for my clients to answer, "Yes," when asked if a family member also suffers or suffered from fears. For some of my clients, it only becomes apparent during the course of our conversation that a family member must have had fears, as it often wasn't discussed aloud around them when they were young.

A good example of this transmission mechanism is arachnophobia (fear of spiders), a fairly common phobia. The truth is, I have never had a client who cited a traumatic experience with a spider as the trigger for their fear of them. Typically, there's no explanation for this fear, other than that it has just always been that way. Some of my clients believed in the theory that arachnophobia is an innate human fear of spiders. However, I always counter that by pointing out that arachnophobia can be resolved in a single therapy session, so there is no case for it as an evolutionary phobia. This is supported by clients then recalling that one of their parents also didn't like sharing a room with a spider. Sometimes I will then hear, "That's right, my mother once mentioned that she used to be afraid of spiders. But she isn't anymore."

Most fear has its roots in your past.

Fear arises when we feel like we cannot control a situation, and this lack of control may be something we experience early in our lives. As babies, we learn that we have little influence over our surroundings. If we grow up in unstable conditions—for example, if our relationship with our closest family members is not secure—we often face vague fear even in adulthood.

What Happens to Untreated Fear?

The problem with any fear is that it will tend to become chronic and spread. Initially, you might have a fear of heights, but later find yourself struggling to drive over bridges. Eventually, you might develop a fear of driving in general. Therefore, it's crucial to address emerging fear as soon as possible. A very important note: our brains don't differentiate much between imagining something and having it actually happen. In both scenarios, our brains react similarly and trigger similar processes within us.

People with chronic fears often think about the things that scare them. As soon as they imagine a trigger for their fear, their brains and bodies respond with physical symptoms of anxiety. For instance, a patient with arachnophobia might start showing symptoms just by thinking about going to the basement to fetch drinks, fearing the potential presence of spiders there, even though they have not actually gone downstairs.

The Influence of the Subconscious

Diana, the rider who had fallen from her gelding and was now afraid of her mare, felt a sensation every time she rode that she couldn't name. When I worked with her in a state of hypnotic trance, we discovered it was a feeling of being abandoned. As a child, she once woke up from a nightmare and realized she was alone, because nobody came when she screamed. She searched the apartment for her parents, but they were nowhere to be found. She became terribly afraid that her parents had left her and would never return. Somehow, this feeling now surfaced in connection with her fear of her mare. Decades and countless situations where she had felt abandoned lay in between.

Diana's current fear arose from overwhelming emotions, because her subconscious had finally had enough. Our subconscious lets fear arise as a control mechanism, ensuring we avoid certain situations. In this case, Diana's fear developed to try to prevent her from feeling abandoned anymore. Fear and avoidance can kick in when it comes to things like exam anxiety, fear of riding, and more. Usually this works perfectly, because the subconscious has a good reason to allow fear. Those who are afraid avoid what is frightening to them, which ensures they don't have to feel that unpleasant feeling (in Diana's case, the feeling of being abandoned) again. It's actually quite cleverly orchestrated by the subconscious—or it would be, if not for the conscious mind continuing to dwell on the fear. Once that fear is established in the conscious mind, we are focused on the fear itself, and not the unpleasant emotions underlying it. Then we start trying to avoid everything that triggers our fear, thereby solidifying it.

But how can we explain what happens in between the cause and the trigger of the fear?

I believe that every person has something like a personal "fear pitcher." For some, it's large, with room for several gallons, and fills up slowly. For others, it is small, and fills quite quickly. The size of your fear pitcher depends on a variety of factors, such as if someone in your immediate environment, like your parents or grandparents, struggled with fear. If they did, your fear pitcher is likely inherently smaller than that of someone who wasn't exposed to such fear. Whether you were aware of your parents' fears as a child doesn't matter. As Sigmund Freud said, "Subconscious minds communicate with each other." You sensed the fears of those around you, and learned that fear is an appropriate response. It doesn't matter if the object of that fear is the same. If your father was afraid of spiders, you are susceptible to developing a chronic fear, too—whether that fear is about spiders or riding is actually irrelevant.

If your parents were very protective and quick to worry about you, and they prevented you from trying things they thought were dangerous, your fear pitcher may be relatively small. You learned as a child that the world is a dangerous place, and so you are quick to be afraid. Insecure attachments also cause your fear pitcher to be smaller, and as a result of these things, your pitcher fills up more quickly. I'd like to point out, however, that none of this means your parents are to blame for your fear, unless they abused you. Parents usually strive to do their best for their children, and those doing their best, in my view, cannot be at fault.

As for your personal fear pitcher, it fills up over the course of your life. Every time you feel out of control or unable to gain control over a situation, that emotion is poured into your pitcher. Your subconscious matches all situations with feelings, and so all situations with an unpleasant feeling also go into this pitcher. Over the years, this pitcher gets filled. Eventually, one last situation is poured in, it overflows, and this situation becomes the trigger for your fear. For Diana, the fall from the gelding was the situation that ultimately triggered her fear, even though the cause was in her childhood.

We become the stories we tell ourselves. In order to change ourselves, it's helpful to change our narratives about ourselves, because our subconscious understands and lives by these stories. One of the great masters of hypnosis, Milton Erickson, understood that we need to change our stories to change ourselves and our lives, and trance—an altered state of attention central to hypnosis—is the easiest way to do it.

What Happens in the Brain

I won't overload you with a lot of technical neuro-biology, but there's some key information that can explain certain connections for you, and it will help if you know about it.

The brain is divided into regions, some of which are responsible for unconscious processes and informa-tion, and others of which handle conscious ones. One of these regions, the limbic system, is responsible for many unconscious processes. Evolutionarily speaking, the limbic system is a very old part of the brain.

One of the most interesting parts of the brain is the amygdala. The amygdala is part of the limbic system and plays a role in the formation of emotions, especially fear and anxiety. It is also involved in the storage of emotionally charged memories. The fron-tal cortex exerts strong control over the amygdala, which is why emotions, including fear, can be sup-pressed to some extent. Fear cannot be completely suppressed, however, as this emotion is necessary to ensure our survival.

Next to the amygdala is the hippocampus, which also belongs to the limbic system and is the archive for our memories. There, memories can be timestamped and stored.

An evolutionarily more recent part of our brain is the prefrontal cortex. This part is responsible for logical, rational thoughts, and when we talk about our con-sciousness, we often mean this area. With our pre-frontal cortexes, we plan our days, try to come up with solutions, and often rely on logical insights.

Fight, Flight, or Freeze Response

Imagine this: It's a beautiful summer day, and you've brought your horse back to the pasture. It's too warm to really do anything, so you've just groomed him and spent some time with him. Birds are chirping, and you feel a gentle breeze on your skin. You remove the horse's halter and set him free. Everything is peaceful and serene. But then, suddenly, your horse panics. He begins to kick, and veers toward you unexpectedly. You just barely jump out of the way in time, and from a safe distance, you realize he almost ran you over in his panic. You see him sprinting wildly across the pasture, still pausing occasional-ly to buck and kick. Out of range, you can feel your tension slowly dissipating. Just a moment ago, your muscles were tense, your heart was beating faster than usual, and you were probably breathing hard. You wonder what got into your horse.

Does this scene sound familiar to you? If so, you prob-ably live in an area where there are deer flies! Indeed, this was how my horse Gitano and I first encountered one. He was beside himself and was not aware of me at all at that moment. I don't know what would have happened if I had paused to think before jumping out of the way. I probably wouldn't have been able to dodge him in time.

Fortunately, my body's alarm system saved me—my amygdala. Your amygdala assesses all external stim-uli, and when it detects danger, "fight or flight" mode is activated. Immediately, a flood of stress hormones, adrenaline, noradrenaline, and cortisol are released, preparing the body for flight or fight.

The heart beats faster, and breathing accelerates to provide the major muscle groups in the arms and legs with more oxygen-rich blood. The muscles there tense up, ready for action. You start to sweat, and may feel a tingling in your stomach—or perhaps your hands turn cold. All of this happens almost instantaneously, and fortunately for us, this fear reaction is faster than our

Just exuberance?

conscious perception of the trigger that set it off. This speed can be a potentially life-saving advantage.

Interestingly, several non-essential organs and parts of the brain reduce their function during this reaction phase. Remember the prefrontal cortex? It's one of the parts that goes offline during extreme danger, because the release of noradrenaline inhibits its activity in stressful situations. This shuts off overthinking and analysis—which is useful, since taking the time to weigh all your options could delay an appropriate reaction long enough to get you killed. As you can see from the example scenario, it's vital that we are able to react automatically in moments of genuine danger, without weighing the pros and cons of various courses of action (even if it leads to "unthinking" responses).

When neither flight nor fight is possible in the face of a threat, but the body's stress system is fully activated, the organism falls into a state of paralysis—this state is called "freeze." In this state, you can't act, flee, or fight. This freezing is akin to the animal kingdom's instinctive fear paralysis—"playing dead." You let what's happening happen, because there appears to be no other option.

The problem with all of this is that the human brain doesn't distinguish between imagined and real events, so just imagining danger can trigger the body's alarm system. If you imagine your horse throwing you off during a jump, you immediately feel uneasy and start to experience the typical physical symptoms of fear. Unfortunately, these physical symptoms also tend to inhibit your ability to ride.

Whenever your brain switches to fight, flight, or freeze mode while you're on a horse, your posture deteriorates, regardless of whether the danger is real or imagined. Your muscle tension increases, especially in the large muscle groups in your arms and legs. Then, because of this rigidity in your buttocks and thighs, you lift yourself out of the saddle, sitting "above the horse" rather than "with the horse." You can't follow his motion smoothly. It's likely you'll also lean forward, because under stress we instinctively want to curl up and protect our internal organs.

Additionally, due to increased muscle tension in your arms, you can no longer gently hold or release the reins; instead, you can only grip them tightly. You can't give clear aids with any part of your body anymore. As the ride goes on, you may freeze on your horse in the face of danger (real or imagined), as your brain realizes there's no point in fighting or fleeing. Nothing really happens to save the situation. You remain frozen and incapable of action, until either you fall off, or the danger has passed and you can shakily dismount.

You can't turn off this alarm system in your body. Even if it were possible, it wouldn't be a good idea, since you do need it to survive real danger. However, it is possible to change your thoughts, assessments, and the things you imagine, when it comes to what constitutes danger in the subconscious and therefore also in the limbic system.

Remember, the conscious part of your mind, the prefrontal cortex, can't do much when it's offline in a frightening situation, so you can't make any conscious considerations during moments of fear. But by figuring out what triggers your fear, you can gain control by changing the perception of fear in your subconscious and bypassing your limbic system's response.

You're probably starting to see that it's crucial to know where your fears come from and why your body reacts the way it does when you're scared. Another thing to consider with respect to your fears is what happens mentally. I'll discuss this further in the next section.

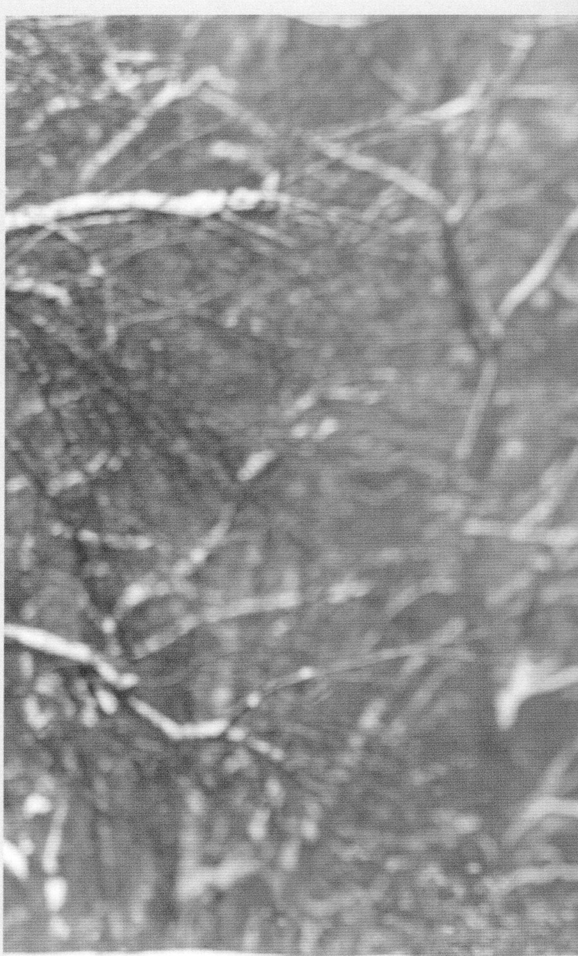

Fear affects your posture, and your ability to give aids.

The Cause Behind The Cause

As you've probably already noticed, fear almost always originates in the feeling of losing control. This feeling of not being able to control our environment is something most of us experience very early in our lives. Many of us encounter this as toddlers, for instance, when we can't influence whether we get food or not, whether we are comforted or not, or whether we feel alone.

In fact, for most of the people I've worked with, the feeling of being alone or abandoned is a primary cause of any anxieties that develop later in life. These principal sources of anxiety are the most common, followed closely by stressors originating in feelings of being overwhelmed or not being good enough. You may be wondering how I came to this conclusion, so let me explain briefly: When I use hypnosis to work with clients on their fears, I employ the technique of regression to identify the root cause of the problem. Invariably, we end up in some childhood situation where my client first felt as they do now regarding horse riding. At the moment of its inception, this feeling of fear is usually much less intense, but over the years, it grows stronger. I'll illustrate this with an example from my practice.

Most fears originate in childhood.

My client Ulrike was in her mid-fifties and had only recently started riding horses when she came to me. She had a reliable horse and felt fairly safe doing trail rides, even though she knew her riding wasn't very steady.

At some point, though, her horse was startled during a trail ride and bucked briefly. Ulrike's unstable seat meant she had trouble staying mounted during her horse's sudden movement, and she felt afraid in that moment, as well as during later outdoor rides. Moreover, Ulrike's horse began bucking repeatedly during trail rides, instilling so much fear in her that she had avoided riding outside for some time.

When our sessions first began, I met Ulrike at the barn with her mare, Fee. I wanted to observe Fee because I believe that a horse doesn't buck without reason. After some discussion, I noticed that Fee was becoming increasingly agitated due to Ulrike's nervousness. This agitation subsided when Ulrike went to fetch her saddle. But when she returned with it, Fee pinned her ears back. When I asked if Fee always did this, Ulrike denied it. I asked Ulrike to set the saddle aside for a moment, and then asked if I could touch Fee. With Ulrike's permission, I gently ran my hand over Fee's back and discovered that the horse showed sensitivity around the lumbar spine area. I carefully placed the saddle on Fee and saw that it was too long for her back, which explained Fee's sensitivity. I discussed the issue with Ulrike, and we tried another saddle, which fit much better. Ulrike was shocked, especially since the first saddle had recently been re-flocked. She quickly wanted to call a saddle fitter and also make an appointment with an equine osteopath.

After our onsite meeting, Ulrike and I went to her home to approach her fear problem through hypnosis.

During hypnosis, we unearthed the root cause of her anxiety, which led us back to a childhood event. In this memory, she was learning to ride a bike that was too large for her. She felt unbalanced and overwhelmed, but the adults around her made her feel as if she simply wasn't trying hard enough, and she was scolded. So she practiced alone and fell, for which she was reprimanded again. We addressed this memory and discussed it afterward. Ulrike was surprised that the root of her current fear was this seemingly unrelated childhood event. However, she recognized that she was grappling with the same emotions that she had felt back then with the bike, even though her current feelings weighed much more heavily on her.

Ulrike contacted me some time later to let me know that she felt that her relationship with Fee had improved. Ulrike was conscious of a change within herself, and realized that her fear was diminishing. After the saddle was correctly fitted and the equine osteopath treated Fee, nothing stood in the way of their rides together. They both still immensely enjoy hitting the trails, without any bucking incidents.

If you have a horse that bucks, rears, or bolts, it's natural to be afraid. Your subconscious fundamentally wants the best for you, and it especially wants to keep you safe from harm. One of the most powerful ways it does this is by inducing fear in you. However, it would be negligent to only address the rider's fear, without also looking for other possible reasons behind the horse's behavior.

ADDITIONAL CAUSES OF FEAR

When discussing fear, we typically assume it stems from psychological causes. However, there are also physical illnesses that can give rise to fear, or that can amplify existing fears. I'd like to mention a few of these diseases here, partly because I am personally affected by one of them, and partly because I've encountered numerous clients with these conditions and have made fascinating observations in this area.

I suffer from a chronic immune system disease called Hashimoto's. The complete name is Hashimoto's autoimmune thyroiditis. Hashimoto's is an autoimmune disorder where the body's immune system no longer recognizes the thyroid as part of the body, and starts to fight it as if it were a foreign entity. In the process, the thyroid is gradually converted from hormone-producing tissue to connective tissue. As a result, fewer thyroid hormones are produced, leading to hypothyroidism. This condition may result in symptoms such as tiredness, abnormal weight gain, depression, and muscle aches, among others.

An almost opposite condition is Graves' disease, which typically results in hyperthyroidism. The bulk of the symptoms of Graves' disease are caused by an excessive production of hormones by the thyroid gland. These symptoms may include, but are not limited to: a racing heartbeat, hand tremors, trouble sleeping, weight loss, muscle weakness, neuropsychiatric symptoms, and heat intolerance.

If your thyroid produces too many or too few hormones, it can have massive effects on your body and your psyche. It's not uncommon for this to cause anxiety, or to exacerbate existing anxieties. Sadly, in my practice, I often observe that thyroid patients are not adequately medicated and have not achieved a medication dosage that allows them to feel their best. If you suspect or know you have a thyroid condition, I advise seeking treatment from an endocrinologist and informing yourself about the disease. This includes determining at which point within the normal blood range you feel best. There are now many doctors who do more than just apply the standard treatment. If you want to learn more, you can find information on my website: www.equihypnosis. com/post/when-the-thyroid-rides-along/

Hormones in general have a profound influence on our emotional lives. If you have other hormonal issues, or if you are on hormonal contraceptives and don't tolerate birth control pills well, this might be reflected in your fears. Additionally, gluten or histamine can lead to or intensify fears, if you are intolerant to these substances. This is especially worth checking if your fear fluctuates significantly and you have phases of feeling very good or very bad. While there could be other reasons for this, if you notice such fluctuations, consider whether your diet might be a factor.

Regardless of their source, this book offers various solutions to address your fears and move past them.

THE STORY OF YOUR FEAR

You've already learned a lot about the theoretical backgrounds of your feelings and your fear. However, it's also important for you to confront your personal situation. For many riders, riding fear stems from an unpleasant experience related to horses, but as you now know, this is only part of the picture. It also matters whether your fear is solely related to riding, or if it occurs when you are simply interacting with a horse, or if fear is a constant companion in other areas of your life. Many of my clients struggle with fear during riding, but are hindered by anxiety in other contexts, too.

Many riders are also afraid of other things.

Common fears many people shared, riders included, are: fear of heights, fear of driving, fear of elevators, and fear of flying, as well as other fears and sometimes even panic attacks. Do any of those sound familiar? Perhaps, as you were reading, you were mentally formulating a list of your own fears. If you experience any of these (or other) fears, the following exercises and self-hypnosis methods will help you with these anxieties, too, not just your riding anxieties.

This is because most fears have a common origin from which they've gradually developed. For this reason, it's sensible to address all fears as you work through this book. To get started, answer the following questions to understand your current state.

Current state—Riding fear:
- What exactly are you afraid of?
- What doesn't scare you when it comes to riding?
- What works well, and at what point does riding become challenging?
- What physical symptoms do you experience when you are fearful?
- How would you describe your horse: Is he fearful or brave?
- Is your horse only anxious around you, or does he also respond with similar levels of nervousness or fear around other people?
- What have you done so far to address your fears?
- What has helped?
- Does your coach/trainer support you?
- Do you know someone who can assist you with the exercises in this book? (You should trust this person, and they should be able to refrain from giving unsolicited advice.)
- What do you want to achieve? What is the goal you want to reach in your riding, with the help of this book?

Current state—Other fears:
- Are there other fears in your life that limit you? What are they?
- Which fear appeared first and how long have you had it?
- How have your fears evolved?

- What have you done so far to combat them?
- What has helped you so far?
- Would you generally describe yourself as a fearful person?
- Do you have any chronic diseases or other psychological disorders? (If you have any chronic diseases, it's essential to be under the care of a specialist and receive adequate treatment.)
- Do you regularly take medications? How about hormonal contraceptives?
- How do you feel in general?
- How well do you sleep? Do you have sleep issues?
- Do you tend to dwell on or overthink things?
- Are you satisfied with your life, your job, and your relationships?
- Are you currently under a lot of stress?
- Do you have support from friends, family, and loved ones?
- Are there things you'd like to change? What do you want to achieve? Phrase this as a positive statement (focused on what you do want, not what you want to avoid) to set a goal for yourself.
- What do you envision for your future?

Once you've answered and analyzed these questions, you'll know whether you can use this book primarily for conquering riding fear or for other problems as well. The more space fear occupies in your life, the more exercises you will need. Don't worry—none of the exercises take a lot of time. But be sure to read the entire book first, and then implement the exercises in your daily life to manage all your fears.

What Your Horse Wants to Tell You

You and your horse share a relationship. You've probably heard many times that this relationship is as it should be when your horse sees you as the boss and feels safe with you. You might conclude from this that you need to be dominant for your horse to feel secure. However, science sees it differently, and so do I. This book isn't about horse training or learning behavior, so I'll address this part only briefly. If you're interested in finding out more, there are references for good books for further reading in the bibliography (page 133).

Your horse knows you're a human and not part of his herd. A herd refers to a group of horses that have familial relationships with each other, and in the wild, horses naturally form these herd groupings. By contrast, the groupings we impose on our horses in a barn or stable make them a jumbled bunch—using a kind of shared living space—with members changing more or less frequently, which is not at all the same as a herd of horses in nature, even though we often refer to such groups of animals as "herds." The behavior of wild horses and domesticated horses is therefore very different. Conflicts are rare in a well-structured herd. There's plenty of space to avoid conflicts, in nature, and since wild horses in the same herd generally belong to one breed, there are no communication issues due to differences in breed and upbringing. Therefore, subtle signals are usually sufficient as a means of communication between individual herd members, and rough manners are usually unnecessary.

Horses also take out stress on other horses.

In the group housing situation provided by humans, however, there is often not enough space, so horses can't avoid each other. And because the members of the group change more frequently, a reliable structure with continuity is rare. This leads to stress in individual horses, and horses, like humans, tend to take their stress out on others.

It is now known that horses don't have as fixed a hierarchy in their herds as was previously assumed. Horses have different roles and tasks, just like humans, and these may change from time to time. So it's not that the higher-ranking horse always has the say and forcefully asserts himself. On the contrary, good leaders among horses are calm, punish little, and often avoid conflicts.

In horse training, you often hear the phrase, "You need to show him who's boss." Such statements are frequently accompanied by physical measures to dominate the horse. These are then justified by claiming that this is how horses naturally interact with each other. Examples such as fights between stallions competing for a group of mares or shifts in authority in artificially grouped horses are used. Upon closer inspection, however, it's clear that none of these examples hold true under normal circumstances, and they certainly don't justify physically disciplining a horse to "show him who's boss."

Consider this: your horse can feel a fly on his coat, so he doesn't need massive (or even moderate) physical pressure to understand signals. Also, we all learn best when it's worth our while to do so, and this applies to you as well as to your horse. In fact, horses (and most animals in general) can be very effectively motivated with food. Opponents of this type of training believe that food rewards lead to poorly trained horses. They believe that you're manipulating the horse with the food, or the horse isn't really responding positively for the owner but is just after the food.

I'd like to counter this with: If you work with negative reinforcement (pressure and the release of pressure), the result is the horse only doing something so that something unpleasant stops—the pressure is released. If you work with punishment, the horse will want to avoid it. This can also lead to learned helplessness. Exercising dominance is certainly a worse motivator than positively reinforcing behavior with food. While there are other methods of positive reinforcement, food is generally a high-quality reinforcement. The question, then, is whether your horse loves you more when he associates you with something unpleasant (pressure or positive punishment) or something pleasant (food, positive reinforcement).

In this case, horse and human like each other.

Lastly, I'd like to address the argument that food rewards result in unruly horses. If you give food rewards correctly and consistently, right after the behavior you want to reinforce, you won't turn your horse into a cookie monster. Working with positive reinforcement is more about training yourself to reinforce what you want, appropriately and at the right time. People commonly use a mix of different strategies to shape behavior, but you should always think about how the horse will feel in response to a particular strategy you want to use. I always advise people to throw in a lot of positive reinforcement, and not to use punishment, as they don't actually go together.

If you want to delve further into modern and scientific horse training, and want to have a motivated and cooperative horse, it's a good idea to stock up on relevant literature regarding learning theory and its use in horse training. Also, find a reputable trainer who knows how to use positive reinforcement without punishment.

Here, horse and human have discovered something worrisome. Who is mirroring whom?

Returning to the idea that your horse should feel safe with you—yes, your horse needs security. You can provide this security by being predictable. A large part of this means taking good care of yourself and regulating your emotions. The most important thing, however, is that you are congruent. In this context, congruence means your external self matches your inner self—you are not trying to pretend to be anything, or hiding your fears, or anything like that. A primary goal of this book is to help you be congruent, and you'll learn more about this in the next chapter.

How Your Horse Reacts To Your Fear

Depending on the personality of your horse, how well you match each other, and how well he can compensate for you, his behavior will vary. We must also not overlook additional factors for both of you, such as health, suitable equipment, and general living conditions. Let's look at the different behaviors your horse might show toward you in certain situations, and what should and should not be done to manage this behavior.

Your Horse Sees Ghosts Everywhere

If you own a very skittish horse, it is essential to figure out whether he has always been skittish, or if his skittishness appeared suddenly. If the skittishness began at a defined point, and your horse also shows it when he is with other people, you should discuss it with your veterinarian. Also, consider: Is the horse consistently skittish, or is he only that way around certain people? The question then becomes—is your horse naturally skittish, or do you make him nervous? As discussed previously in the context of humans, illness can also cause changes in behavior in horses.

Once your horse's health has been checked and you are sure this is not the issue in his case, examine whether there are any other stressors. Do his saddle, bridle, and bit fit correctly? Are all of his needs being met—does he get enough forage and unrestricted access to water? Does he have shelter from the weather, and companions he gets along with? Does he have enough space to actively and easily move around? If you can answer all these questions satisfactorily, then there is something else preventing your horse from feeling relaxed.

If the above criteria are met and your horse is still skittish, it is advisable to have your horse treated osteopathically. Movement restrictions or pain mean stress for all living beings. The former often manifests as tension, irregular gait, resistances, and also skittishness. Stress causes us to react much more strongly to external stimuli than when there is no stress. The horse, as a flight animal, will thus react much more skittishly than usual when he is already stressed. When we are in pain, everything tends to get on our nerves much more quickly. We are, quite literally, more sensitive, and may lose our tempers more quickly or feel attacked more swiftly. The horse is the same way.

To determine whether your horse is mirroring you or displaying his own skittishness, you should first find a relaxed and, above all, unbiased person to interact with your horse. While this person is engaging with your horse, all other individuals should step back and maintain a distance of at least thirty feet to ensure the horse is not reacting to anyone else's presence. After this, if you have determined that the horse himself is skittish and is not mirroring anyone, involve a trainer who is calm themselves, and who trains rather than dominates. Let this trainer work with your horse, and continue training under their supervision if at all

Horses can learn to overcome their suspicion of unfamiliar objects.

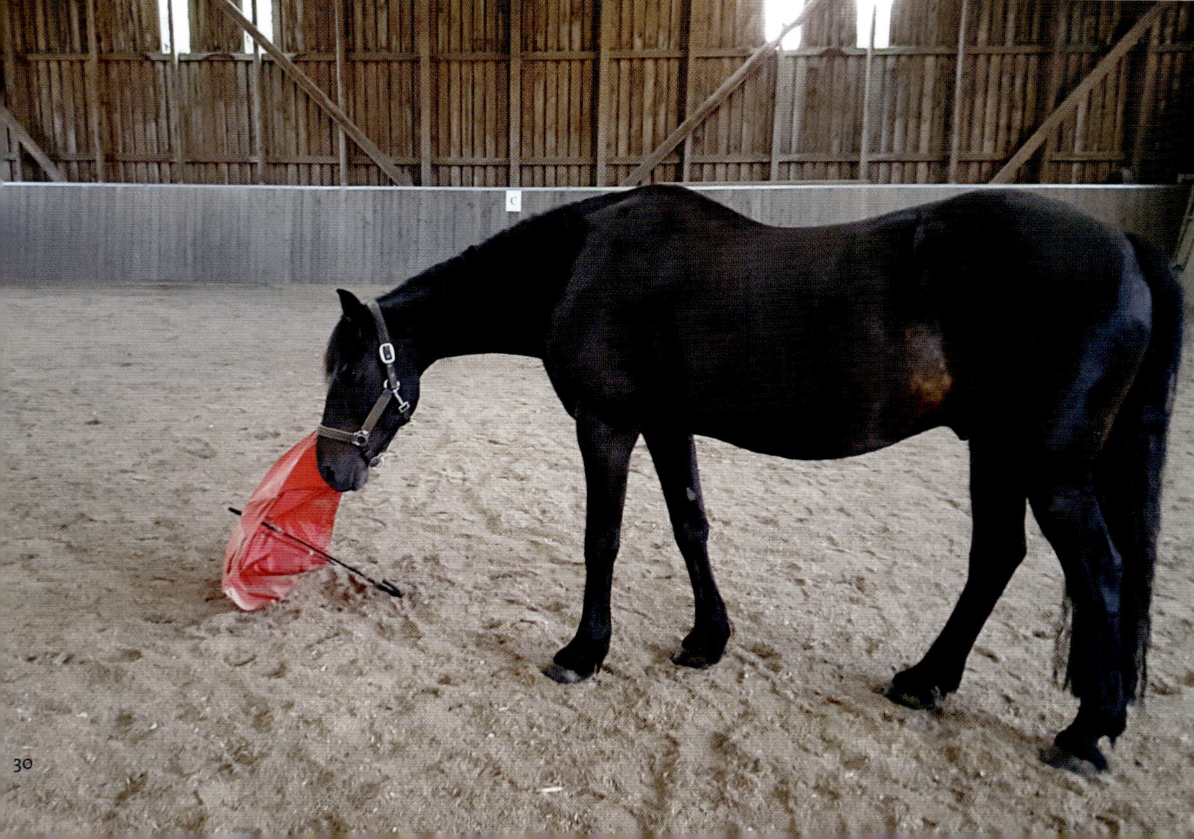

Maybe the horse has a valid reason for his behavior?

possible. There are not as many trainers who work with mindfulness and positive reinforcement in the horse field as there are in the dog field, unfortunately, but if you delve a little into the topic, you will find out what you should look for in a trainer. I also encourage you to research learning behavior in horses and learning theory in general, because the more you know, the more enjoyable the learning and training experience will be for both you and your horse. You'll both be unlearning old and less beneficial habits, in a good and productive way.

Your Horse Bucks, Rears, or Bolts

Fundamentally, I agree with German dressage trainer Egon von Neindorff, who said, "If your horse makes a mistake, look for the cause in yourself. And if you don't find it, search more thoroughly."

Essentially, you are more likely to be at fault than your horse when something isn't working out. Horses are not manipulative or trying to give you a hard time, though this is what we may be led to believe. In my riding career, I have often heard something like, "The horse just wants to mess with you." Horses are sometimes even accused of being malicious, or just plain bad, when they are truly only trying to communicate with us. When you think about it, being "mean" or manipulative doesn't make biological sense for a horse. Horses are primarily prey animals; they conserve their energy so they can run if they need to and are not aggressive predators, so they aren't going to waste effort on pointless pranks. They only defend themselves when escape is not possible.

In most cases, therefore, if a horse bites, kicks, bucks, rears, or bolts, he has a legitimate reason for doing so. He is not doing it to just annoy you. Horses communicate subtly, and, because they are prey animals, they hide pain and discomfort as long as possible so as not to appear to be an easy target for predators. When a horse "acts out," we often misunderstand his behavior, and don't treat it as the cry for help that it is.

Horses do not have many ways to communicate with us, and since we often overlook their subtle signals, they have to amplify certain behaviors to make us see and understand that something is not right. Overall, I'd say that horses endure a lot in silence, and only show us something is wrong when it has been wrong for a long time. It often makes me wonder how much horses bear for the sake of their owners and riders. For instance, a horse will allow himself to be ridden even though his back hurts because the saddle does not fit correctly. Of course, this is not intentional on the part of the rider, because we try to do our best for our horses. We rely on experts like saddle fitters or trainers to help us purchase a saddle, and are later horrified when we find that, in the worst case, the custom saddle does not fit the horse correctly. And that's just one example.

When a horse has to resort to actions like kicking, biting, bucking, rearing, or bolting, he often has a physical problem. If you encounter displays of negative behavior from your horse, the first thing you should do is always check his health and make sure all of his tack fits properly. If he is already pinning his ears back when you approach him with the saddle, this is a clear sign that the saddle does not fit properly. If your horse has stomach problems, he may resist when being girthed. If you notice something like this, respond immediately by checking your equipment and talking to your veterinarian. If you ignore these kinds of signals, your horse will have to take more explicit actions to make you understand.

Of course, a horse can also learn that he can end an unpleasant situation if he bucks, rears, or bolts. However, it goes without saying that you should give your horse the benefit of the doubt and exclude possible causes for these actions that stem from care, health, or equipment. It also makes sense to consult an equine osteopath in these cases. Some horses buck when their backs hurt, others rear, and others run away from the pain. It is also essential to determine whether your horse shows this behavior only with you or with others as well.

When all other possible causes for the unwanted behavior are excluded, and the horse mainly shows this behavior with you, the logical conclusion is that his behavior must have something to do with you. Horses rear, for instance, when pressure through the bridle increases and they have no possibility of escape, or are held back very tightly. If there is no relief from this kind of pressure, some horses will then lean on the bit and bolt. In such cases, we must understand why the horse does what he does, and how you can influence his behavior. As I've described here, for riders dealing with a rearing or bolting horse, the cause is usually a very rigid and hard hand. This is no surprise, when fear is involved. As you already know, when in a state of fear, the rider's muscles will tense, and she will start holding the reins tightly.

If your horse rears or bolts, it is essential to proceed in small steps and apply everything I will convey to you in the following chapters. If the horse shows this behavior with every rider, and you've entirely ruled out a physical reason for it, it may also be learned behavior. The good news is that the horse can unlearn this behavior. In this case, it is best to find a mindfully positive trainer with whom you can tackle the problem.

Your Horse Is Totally Cool

Are you constantly on edge, waiting for your horse to

Sometimes you're the one who's nervous—whereas even the thundering train passing by doesn't unsettle your horse.

flinch, but the only thing that moves abruptly is his ear? Are you expecting a random outburst from your horse, even though he is an absolutely balanced and good-natured animal?

Do you know very well that your fear is unfounded, but you cannot switch it off? You are not alone. Many riders are afraid to ride their horses even though the horses are absolutely sound and otherwise very chill. In these cases, there is usually a deeper reason why the rider feels fear. If this is you, be patient with yourself—and be happy that your horse is not giving you additional reasons to be afraid. You are actually very lucky, because your horse is able to compensate for your insecurity and fear, and this will allow you to concentrate fully on yourself. In the next chapters, you will learn how you can regulate yourself and influence your fear. Believe me, nobody has to live with fear. If you get the feeling that you need personal assistance or there is still something for you to work on, do not hesitate to seek help.

You Only Have This Problem With Your Horse

I know some riders who have an impasse because riding their own horses feels like an impossible task. In many cases, this difficulty arises when the horse and rider haven't known each other for very long. Often, the horse was acquired when he was very young and inexperienced, even though he might already have been started under saddle. When the new rider was trying him out, he was a very brave young horse—calm, confident, and full of promise.

However, when the horse was brought into his new environment, that good-natured composure seemed to vanish. The rider quickly has her first doubts: Was I mistaken? Is this horse not so calm after all? Among stable colleagues, opinions are unfortunately formed very quickly, and before you know it, rumors begin to circulate that the new horse is an unpredictable, chaotic creature that was probably sedated and passed off as well-trained.

A new environment always means stress for the horse, even if it is not immediately apparent.

Comments like these often cause chagrin and embarrassment, in addition to the shame the rider might be feeling because she feels as though she cannot successfully ride her horse. Unfortunately, our riding peers often react with a tactless lack of understanding when someone is afraid of their own horse.

If that scenario wasn't the case with your horse, though, then everything is clearly your fault from the start. You messed up your new horse. I'm only joking, of course. However, there certainly are people who are so nervous that they make even the saintliest horse neurotic (which is not to say you are one of those people). But it is important to realize that entering a new environment is a drastic change, for a horse. Horses are creatures of habit, and it can take months and months for a horse to get used to a new place and adapt to a new owner or rider. What happens during that period of adjustment has a strong impact on the relationship between horse and human, and the psyche of both.

You should be very honest with yourself, if you find that you are only afraid of your own horse. Do you otherwise fit well together? As in the rest of life, we can fall in love with someone who doesn't actually match our personality or fit into our lives. It happens to us with people and with horses. If you learned to ride on a comfortable Fjord and dream of companionable rides at a leisurely walk, but then lose your heart to a spirited but traumatized Iberian, you will have a lot of adjusting to do. Sometimes we lose our hearts quickly, but love is not always enough. Sometimes we have to realize that we want and need something different than our partners can give us—whether they have two or four legs.

If you yourself have experienced hard times, you may naturally feel attracted to horses that have not had it easy—and that's fine. Yes, they can give back a lot. It is wonderful and heartwarming when they give you their trust, and your heart and breathing are in sync. However, the path there is long and crossed by dry spells, and, most importantly, this horse will also be your teacher, and you will have to work hard on yourself. Are you ready? Are you still willing to do everything for this horse, if he doesn't change? Is it okay with you if he finds comfortable rides at the walk miserably boring, and the two of you have to look for another discipline?

If you change, your horse will change—this basic truth cannot be shaken. But the question is: Will the change in your horse be enough of a change for you? Would you be happier with a different personality? With a horse that, like you, enjoys comfortable rambles? These questions and their answers don't mean you have to decide anything today. You bought this book because you hope to find help for yourself—because you want to get rid of your fears. And I am absolutely sure you can succeed. But if you ever notice your horse is simply not the right one for you, it is absolutely okay to let him go. We often hold on to relationships that just don't work for far too long. We put aside any thought of separation. If you feel relief at the thought of finding your horse a new partner, it is an indication that you are not in the right place with this relationship. If you change and your horse changes, but it is not enough for you to feel truly comfortable with him, you owe it to your horse to find him a good new home. It's a hard truth, but one that should be faced.

I myself have two traumatized horses, and I have worked with many riders with traumatized horses. I have seen that it is possible to get rid of your fears, even when the horse continues to have problems with certain things. I have also heard from some riders: "Who would take him the way he is? Either I manage to get along with him, or he will be passed around or turned into sausage." If that's your worry, you will need patience and discipline.

Yes, discipline will be very important for you, because you will have to practice the exercises in this book over and over again. You are also in a more difficult position than, for example, the anxious rider with a calm horse. You can get just as far, but you will have to invest more in yourself and your horse to make it there. Are you ready?

Your Horse Only Has This Problem With You

Here is something very important to consider: Does your horse show fear or defiance only with you? Do other people find your horse as meek as a lamb? Is it only you who says you don't quite trust him? Acknowledging this is not a bad starting point. At least this way, you know that your horse can behave differently, and it's a good indication that he might be mirroring you. You are the problem. This might seem like an unpleasant realization at first, but it is a much easier issue to resolve than if your horse has some other major problem, because you can change yourself. Even if you currently feel at the mercy of your fears, you are not. You can give your life a different direction and improve your sense of security while riding. And then the behavior of your horse will also change.

Chapter 2: How Your Horse Mirrors You

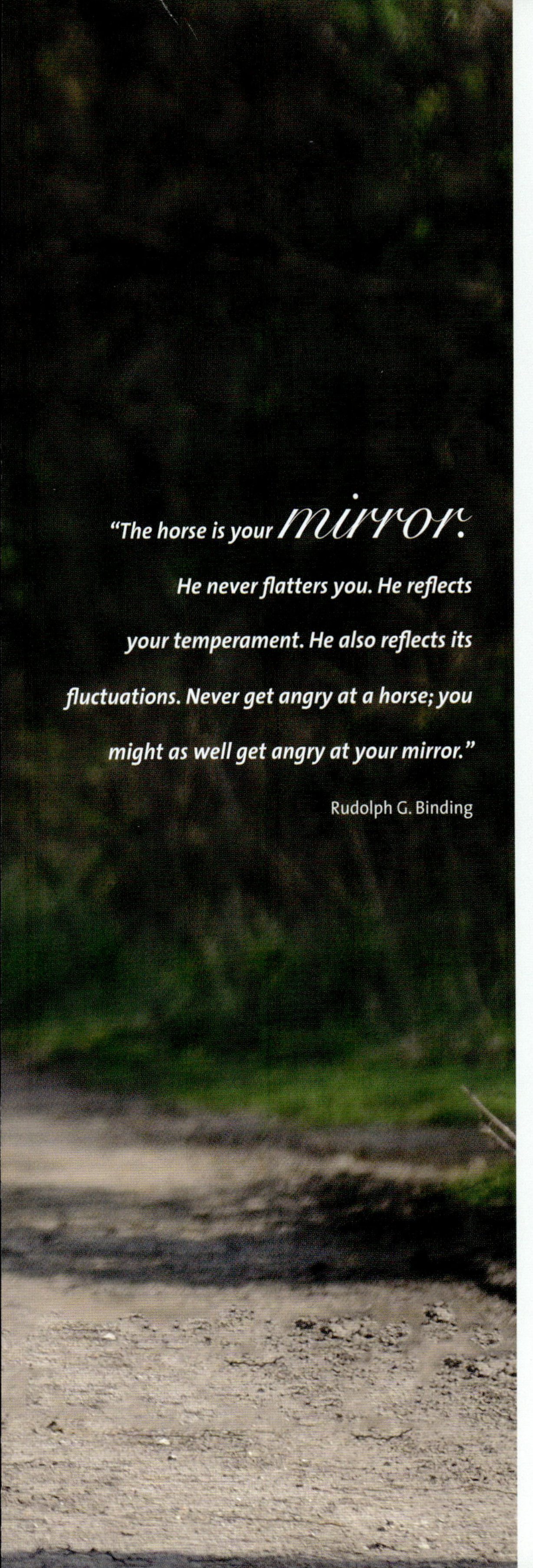

The history of humankind is inextricably entwined with the horse. The horse was and is an animal that has played many fundamental roles in our history. One of these roles is that of a healing entity. Since ancient Greek times, healing or therapeutic abilities have been attributed to horses. Nowadays, we know of numerous horse-supported interventions in which a horse is a (co-)healer or (co-)therapist. These include: hippotherapy, horse-assisted physiotherapy, speech therapy or occupational therapy, horse-assisted learning or coaching, and also horse-assisted psychotherapy.

One reason why riding horses can have a therapeutic effect is that their movement patterns stimulate the human brain hemispheres and our balance system. This movement pattern can also trigger memories and feelings. For example, through body contact with the horse's back, trauma memories related to sexual assaults are often awakened. If you are a victim of sexual violence and intense feelings overwhelm you while you are on a horse's back, this could be one factor contributing to your fear. (I just wanted to mention this topic briefly, even though it goes far beyond the subject of this book, because I encounter the effects of sexual abuse in my practice more often than I would like, and you should be aware of its potential impact.)

Another reason why horses are so commonly used in therapy and coaching is that they mirror humans and are absolutely authentic. Horses mirror us because their responses include what our presence communicates to them. I would like to elaborate on this.

Horses have a therapeutic effect on us.

Why Do Horses Mirror?

———

"Every form of deception is absolutely foreign to the nature of horses and their essence.

Malice and contradictory actions are purely human characteristics."

Susanne Kreuer

The horse, as a prey and flight animal, needs to decide in milliseconds whether or not another creature poses a potential threat. Whether that creature appears dangerous depends on its smell, muscle tone, and breathing. When in doubt, the horse will first choose to flee. His flight distance is usually fairly short, however, and he will soon come to a stop and turn back toward the potential source of danger to take a closer look.

Humans are unique among living beings because we can suppress feelings, repress them, try to pretend we are feeling different feelings than we actually are, and also lie to others. However, these actions still affect our facial expressions, heart rate, breathing, muscle tone, and ultimately our scent. This is why you can't fool or lie to a horse. As a prey animal, the horse looks for congruence, meaning: does what you are showing externally match your inner feelings and what the horse can sense in you? For example, maybe you have just had a fierce argument with your partner and are actually boiling with anger, but you are trying to radiate calm while you are with your horse. This is basically impossible to do well enough that your anger will be truly concealed from your horse, and the incongruence is hard for him to bear or understand.

How difficult this is for your horse depends a lot on his own mental resilience, breed, and experiences. You surely know horses that endure everything with stoic calm and are not easily upset. You probably also know the opposite: a horse that explodes in milliseconds and generally has a very high level of arousal. Such a horse will not be able to compensate for your unconscious feelings much, if at all. By the same token, it's fair to say that there are certain people who radiate calm to every horse, as well as people who can turn even the most reliable horse into a freaked-out, chaotic mess within seconds.

All mammals, including humans and horses, have so-called mirror neurons, a very special type of nerve cell in the brain. Some researchers speculate that it is through our mirror neurons that we are able to empathize with what others are going through, and mimic or reflect their behavior. This process of relating to the behavior of others is instinctive and allows us to experience closeness and group belonging. And, like humans, horses are also highly social beings; mirroring is vital for their survival in a herd. When danger threatens, the herd moves as a unit, because horses mimic each other.

The whole group is relaxed.

It's better to escape together.

What Do Horses Mirror?

———

"Knowledge of the true nature of horses is the first foundation of *horsemanship,* and every rider must make it their main subject."

François Robichon de la Guérinière

It's worth repeating: horses mirror you both physically and emotionally, and they do this by displaying particular physical actions and emotional behaviors. Physical mirroring by your horse is particularly evident when you are riding. If you are not relaxed while sitting on your horse, he will not move in an easy and relaxed manner underneath you. Your horse pays attention to your muscle tension and tries to adapt to it as he continually seeks to find balance with you. It makes sense when you think about it. Have you ever worn a backpack that was very rigid and stiff, and did not move with your body? You probably couldn't walk comfortably with it and felt tense while carrying it. In contrast, a backpack that doesn't restrict you and adjusts to your body's movement allows you to move freely. It is the same with your horse—your rigid muscles make him tense and uncomfortable.

Not every horse reflects a rider's physical tension in the same way, but some horses will mirror tension in specific muscle areas one-to-one. For instance, my Iberian horse reacts strongly to rigidity in my neck muscles. If there is too much muscle tension there, he raises his head high, like a giraffe. Only when I manage to release the tension in my neck does he do the same and drop his head.

Emotional mirroring is also significant, especially in relation to your fear. Horses may mirror your emotions, both those you openly display and those you perhaps unknowingly suppress.

The horse reflects you physically and emotionally.

Typical unconscious emotions include grief and anger, which may be suppressed because in some contexts it is seen as inappropriate to display them. Often, we're not even aware that we're doing it. However, in situations where a horse is being used in a therapy or coaching session, it can become very evident when he is mirroring suppressed emotions, as both grief and anger may manifest in the horse as heightened arousal and a certain level of aggression.

In terms of other suppressed emotions, one emotion we often consciously try to mask is fear. In this case as well, the horse may reveal this hidden emotion through increased arousal levels and growing nervousness.

What Effect Can You Have on Mirroring?

"I will do everything possible and give my best so that these horses, in their friendly nature, think well of me, and so that harmony prevails, supported by the mutual understanding between two beings."

Nuno Oliveira

You should not try to actively influence a horse to mirror you, because you simply don't need to; this type of response is part of his nature. A horse can help you discover and recognize what lies within you, and deserves your respect for that service. Once you are able to confront your suppressed emotions, your horse will no longer need to show you what lies hidden within you.

Your horse is a sensitive animal with needs and feelings, and is most comfortable in the company of other horses within an established group structure. As mentioned previously, I intentionally avoid using the term "herd" here because most horse owners cannot provide their horses with a true herd, which is usually a group of related horses where new members are not always coming and going.

This group of horses has discovered something exciting.

Our horse boarding setups are more like mixed dormitories, with various horse breeds, ages, and genders. Horses come and go, and group membership is not stable or consistent the way it would be in the wild, so there is likely some baseline stress in every domestic horse. But because it does not suit our purposes to allow our horses to live in a more natural state, that makes it even more crucial to ensure that the horse's essential needs for safety, food, and water are met, to minimize his stress as much as possible. Otherwise, you'll never know if your horse's "mirroring" is an actual reflection of you, or is simply the expression of his individual form of "stress" because he is not being kept as a horse should be.

What else is essential to a horse?

You might have noticed that horses in a group pay very close attention to each other. The following scene can often be observed in the pasture: One horse hears a strange noise, raises his head, and looks attentively in the direction of the noise he heard. Then, you also see the other horses' heads snap up. Everyone looks in the same direction. A few continue to graze undisturbed. One of the horses then gives the all-clear by lowering his head, and all the others follow.

If you have a good bond with your horse, mimicking this group behavior is a way to signal to your horse that what he fears poses no danger. Is your horse excited, looking tensely in one direction? Then mirror his behavior. Observe what has caused his excitement, and then signal to him that there is nothing disturbing there by relaxing and calmly carrying on with your business.

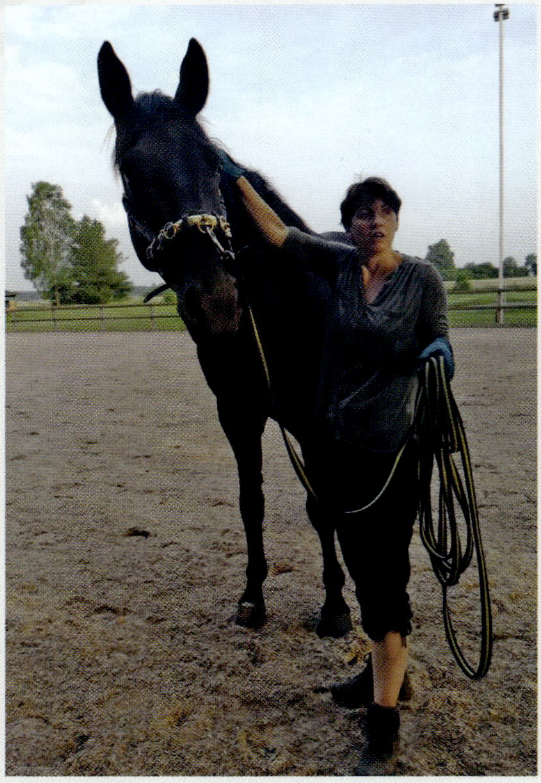

Human mirrors horse...

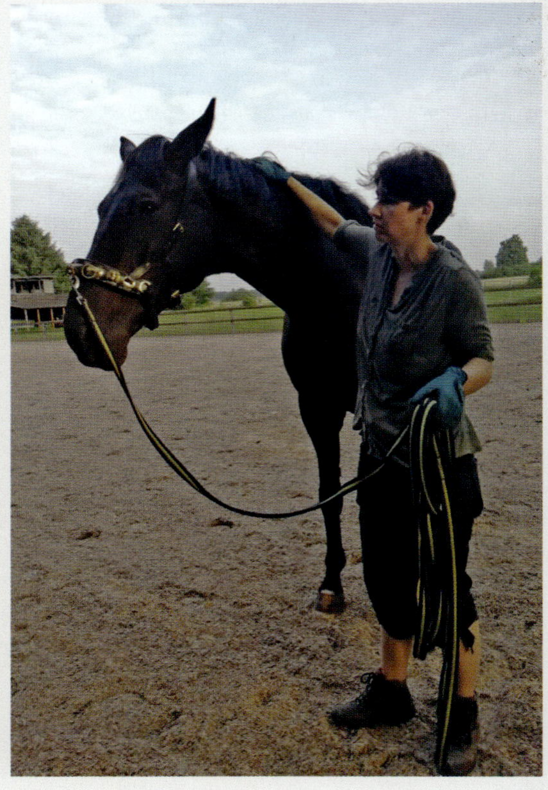

...and horse mirrors human.

 ## How You Mirror Your Horse

Is your horse excited and looking intently in one direction? Straighten up, stare fixedly in the same direction, and hold your breath briefly. Then give the all-clear by exhaling, reducing your muscle tension, and looking somewhere else.

As already mentioned, horses pay attention to breathing and muscle tone, among other things, both with each other and with you. Horses are vigilant creatures, especially because they live in the present. Adult humans, however, often have to relearn this. Mindfulness is key to living in the moment, and thus it is also a way to contain your fears.

Your fears stem from the past. Do you sometimes catch yourself thinking about something bad that has happened to you, remembering a fall or another moment you don't want to experience again? Then you know what I mean when I say that we often live in the past. We spend another part of our time with the future. We imagine what the day will bring, what it will be like the next time we get on a horse—whether everything will go well, or whether we will again not be able to do what our trainers want from us due to fear. Rarely do we live in the present.

A Buddhist parable on mindfulness:

A few seekers came to an old master, and wanted to know how he managed to be happy and satisfied. They said they would like to be as happy as he was.

The master replied: "When I lie down, then I lie down. When I get up, then I get up. When I walk, then I walk, and when I eat, then I eat."

The disciples were a bit disappointed. One said, "What you say, we also do. We sleep, eat, and walk. But we are not happy. So what is your secret?"

The master gave the same answer: "When I lie down, then I lie down. When I get up, then I get up. When I walk, then I walk, and when I eat, then I eat."

The seekers were still dissatisfied with this answer, so after a while, the master added, "Surely you also lie down, and you also walk, and you also eat. But while you lie down, you already think about getting up. While you are getting up, you consider where you are going, and while you are going, you ask yourself what you will eat. Your thoughts are constantly elsewhere and not where you are. Life always takes place in the present. Commit yourself completely to this moment, and you have the chance to be truly happy and satisfied."

How often are you mentally in sync with your horse in what you are both currently doing? Your horse lives in the present. When he eats grass, he isn't thinking about whether you are planning a ride today and whether he will smell a strange dog on the trail again again; he isn't already making himself scared and immediately fleeing in his own thoughts. You, on the other hand, are often far ahead with your thoughts, or, conversely, lagging behind.

When you come to the barn, your thoughts might still be at work, or on what you have to do when you leave the stable. When was the last time you consciously

Horses live in the now.

Am I fully present and conscious with my horse? Or are my thoughts elsewhere?

led your horse? While saddling, you think about riding, and while unsaddling, you're already thinking about your sofa at home, or maybe something else. Do you feel caught out when I say that?

Do you know people who stare at their phones while leading their horses, focused on something else while their horses trail behind them? Or riders who make a call during warm-up or cool-down? They seem to think that this way, they "kill two birds with one stone" because, after all, warming up or cooling down is like wasted time, right?

No, of course it isn't If you want to have a great connection with your horse, if you want him to pay attention to you and respond smoothly to your aids, you should treat your partner with respect and be with him with all your senses, as he is with you. We humans can only do this half as well as horses, so we have to make an effort. But this only works if we practice mindfulness and stay in the present. Only then are you attentive to what is happening; only when you focus on what you're doing can you breathe deeply into your stomach (something horses find very calming). Only then do you gain awareness of your feelings and what lies within you, and only then does your horse not have anything incongruent about you to reveal to you. It is then that your horse no longer needs to obviously mirror you.

I will explain how to become much more mindful in the next section.

Equihypnosis: If You Change, Your Horse Will Change

"No $secret$ *is as deep*

as that between a rider and his horse."

Robert Smith Surtees

I hear repeatedly from clients after just one session with me that their horses have completely changed. My clients are astonished by this, because in these cases, I have only worked on the problems with the client and not also with the horse. The reason for this is that the change has started in the clients themselves, and is showing up in their horses' behavior (which seems quite normal to many riders): When the rider stays calm, the horse has no reason to get upset, and also remains calm. But actually the changes go far beyond that. I would like to give you some examples.

Miriam had repeated problems with her gelding, Tony. Everything began with a ride during which Tony got scared and bolted. She couldn't bring him to a halt, and began to slow him down by turning him in ever smaller circles on a stubble field until he stopped. Totally exhausted, she jumped out of the saddle. But even though Miriam had stayed on in the moment and everything ended well, she still imagined what could have happened if she hadn't been able to stop him. Further ahead was a busy country road, and she played through in her mind how it probably would have ended—in a disaster,

most likely. She led Tony back to the stable in hand, because her knees were still too shaky for her to remount her now calm gelding. She was relieved to arrive safely at the stable, and resolved to bring someone along on the next ride.

Unfortunately, the next ride, this time accompanied, didn't end well either. Tony bolted again, at the same place as last time. Again, it took some time to bring him to a stop, and Miriam couldn't explain at all what the cause was. After a few more riding attempts, during which Tony bolted each time, Miriam wanted to take a break from riding outside and rode in the outdoor arena and indoor. But it was as if her rides were cursed. Tony, who had always had steady nerves before, was increasingly affected by noises and objects that would previously have left him unperturbed. One day, as Miriam was riding Tony in the outdoor arena, a tractor drove along the road. Miriam tensed up, and Tony started to pull. They did a few rounds at a hunting gallop, and Miriam was afraid in every corner that they would slip. Finally, Tony stopped. Since that day, Miriam felt even the outdoor arena wasn't safe, and when I came to work with her, she was riding exclusively in the indoor.

A week after we worked together, Miriam told me that Tony had completely changed. He would neigh when she came, and overall seemed somehow more affectionate. They simply understood each other better, and had already taken a walking trail ride. In the outdoor arena, he hadn't bolted even once.

This was the first time a client told me her horse had transformed after our work. Since then, I have heard this from many of my clients.

Trail riding can be fun.

Your horse will listen to you particularly well when you are in the here and now.

The horses become calmer, more relaxed, don't get upset as quickly, and apparently appreciate it when their humans are willing to work on themselves. It really is true: If you change, your horse will change.

Even small interventions can create a significant change in the horse. In the past, I have been fortunate to have the opportunity to train riding therapists, focusing on equine-assisted psychotherapy and coaching. I have also trained them in hypnosis, and I've found that horses clearly react to a human in hypnosis or self-hypnosis. If the horse avoided the human before the hypnosis, or showed signs of nervousness or stress, then he calmed down significantly when the human was in a state of hypnotic trance. After the hypnosis, the horses reacted more affably and with greater friendliness to people in general. In some cases, they were only interested in a human after that person had undergone hypnosis.

You can make use of the way your horse reflects your progress. You have a training partner by your side who will clearly show you what is working well. Even if you don't feel any positive changes in yourself, if your horse behaves more calmly with you, that's a clear sign that you are getting somewhere. Use your horse as a barometer to judge which exercises are helping you—even if you don't notice anything obvious in yourself.

Some things can change very quickly, and with others, it is a process. It is normal if you don't notice a dramatic change immediately. Often, it takes weeks, during which your subconscious is processing what you initiated in self-hypnosis. By contrast, you will get immediate feedback on exercises you perform with your horse.

All the exercises in the following chapters will positively influence your riding, and especially your seat. Your horse will appreciate that, too. You will notice that he moves more freely under you and that he starts to lengthen his stride. You will be able to play with your imagination to use the exercises for your riding and give your aids more efficiently. Your stability in the saddle will also improve immensely. You will have much greater security if you know you can stay in the saddle even if your horse gets spooked and shies. You will also react more quickly and effectively. So your efforts will definitely be rewarded.

Partners who understand each other.

Part 2

"Our greatest weakness lies in giving up.
The most certain way to succeed is always to try just one more time."
Thomas Alva Edison

Chapter 3: Freeing Yourself from Fear

*H*aving focused mainly on how chronic fear manifests and develops in Part 1, I now want to help you change your fear. You are not defenseless against fear. Rather, you can influence and dissolve it.

Having assessed your fear and its symptoms on a scale (see page 13), you have a way to measure your fear. And when you can measure the intensity of your fear, you can recognize what helps you much more easily. Continuously check how your fear's "scores" change after each of the exercises. This will help you to recognize changes in yourself, so you don't have to rely solely on feedback from your horse.

Surprisingly, we ourselves are often the last to notice changes in ourselves. Once you have assessed your fear, though, this will be easier for you, because you'll have a before-and-after comparison in a shorter time-frame. Otherwise, you might feel as though your fear has only started to significantly decrease after months of work. We often expect changes to show up from one moment to the next. However, changes often occur gradually and progressively in this process—though also more quickly than you might think.

With hypnotic interventions, you work at a very deep level. Changes you initiate have a lasting effect, but it may take some time for them to show up externally in an obvious way. Everything that you can implement on the horse, or in dealing with him on the ground, will also help you in stressful or triggering situations, enabling you to develop further and confront your fear while your subconscious works on the process of change.

If you have not yet quantified your fear and figured out where it lies on the scale I provided, do it now, before you continue reading.

Get in Control

Every type of fear involves the feeling of losing control. With a horse by your side or beneath you, you are interacting with a living being that you cannot always control, so there is always an opportunity for fear to intrude. However, you can always control yourself, your actions, and your reactions, and these influence your horse.

It may be that you react with fear when your horse flinches briefly, because you expect him to shy, and you feel like you might not be able to stay on board. You react to this worry with tension in your body.

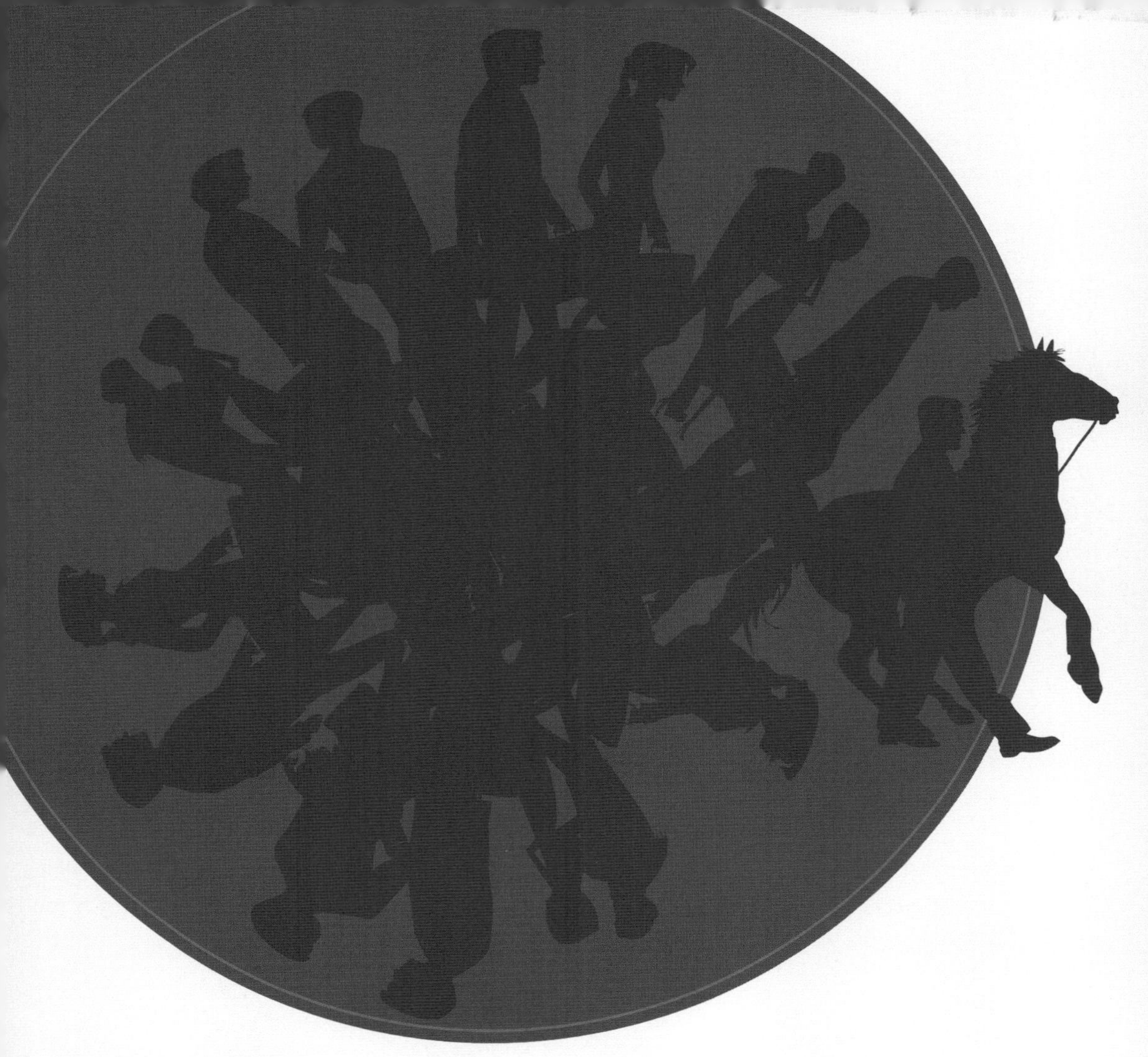

Your breathing becomes shallower; perhaps you also hold your breath. Stress hormones are released, and your muscle tension increases. Your body's center of gravity shifts a bit upward, and you now sit perched "above" your horse. In this mode, you have virtually no control. You have given up your seat, and you can no longer give proper aids.

Since you can't immediately change your horse's behavior, it makes sense to learn to control and change your own. A very crucial point here is breathing. Everything depends on our breathing.

Our life begins with the first breath and ends with the last.

You might know the following exercise if you are familiar with *Centered Riding* by Sally Swift. It is called "Soft Eyes," and together, "Soft Eyes" and correct "Breathing" are two of the four basics of centered riding. Because they are part of the foundation of centered riding, we should always apply them, ensuring that we always ride with "soft eyes" and correct breathing. This exercise is especially important for riders experiencing fear.

EXERCISE: "Soft Eyes"

>>> On the ground, position yourself so that you have a good stance, and your feet are about shoulder-width apart. Slightly bend your knees so that you could bounce a little in your knees if you wanted to.

>>> Now find a point at eye level in front of you, and focus on this point. Stare at it and concentrate entirely on this one point. While doing this, pay attention to how you feel inside your body, and be aware of your breathing. It's important that you keep focusing on that point you chose. Feel whether you are holding your breath or if your breath flows freely; also feel how deep the breath goes. Are you breathing into your chest, or do you feel like you're breathing deep into your belly? Once you've noticed your breathing, let your gaze soften. Without moving your head, keep looking at the point, but allow your field of vision to expand, and don't stare anymore. You might even feel like you're looking beyond the point. You can also perceive what is on either side of you, and what surrounds you. Though you are still looking at the point, you aren't focusing so hard upon it.

>>> While you softly look at the point, check the feeling inside your body again, and notice how you are breathing now.

>>> If you feel like you're breathing a bit more deeply, or your breath is flowing more smoothly, everything is as it should be. We can expand this exercise a bit more and include centering, but first, I'll give you some guidance in case you found the exercise challenging.

Focus on a point.

https://equihypnosis.com/softeyes

You don't feel your breathing:

If you don't feel your breathing, allow yourself to simply observe your breathing. Place your hands on your stomach, and feel how your stomach expands under your hands as you inhale, and how it flattens as you exhale. Try it several times without putting yourself under any pressure to breathe any particular way. We are not used to focusing on our breathing; we usually don't have to think about it. Our breathing is often controlled without any conscious effort, and sometimes it's hard for us to perceive it.

Putting your hands on your lower abdomen helps you perceive your breathing more clearly.

You don't feel a difference between "hard" and "soft" eyes:

If you don't notice a difference in your breathing when you move from sharp focus to "soft eyes," try this: place your hands on your stomach, and feel whether the movement of your stomach with "soft eyes" is any larger. A small difference is enough.

You still don't feel any difference?

If you still don't feel anything, don't worry—you can always come back to this exercise. For now, let's move on to Centering, which often helps.

Centering—The Ball

>>> Continue to stand with your feet about shoulder-width apart. If you want, close your eyes. If you think you might start to sway, or if you feel insecure with closed eyes, choose a point on the ground that is somewhat farther away from you to look at, so that you are looking down without bending your neck.

Centering with closed eyes.

>>> Now imagine that you have a ball or a sphere in your abdomen. This can also be a light or a cloud, if the idea of a ball is uncomfortable for you. Whatever you imagine, it should be pleasant for you and look nice. Now imagine that the ball, sphere, cloud, or light sinks downward in your abdomen—until it comes to rest in your pelvis. Your pelvis is shaped like a bowl, and offers the ball, cloud, or light a nice, secure place to settle. If you were to move, the ball would also move slightly, maybe rocking back and forth a bit. Nevertheless, it is well and safely stored there in your pelvis. This is your center.

>>> While you imagine the ball in your pelvis, open your eyes and look softly forward. How are you breathing now?

>>> Do you feel like you're breathing more deeply? Do you feel more stable?

>>> If not, check the problems and possible solutions.

https://equihypnosis.com/centering

You find it creepy to imagine something in your body:

If you find having something inside you unpleasant to try to visualize, there is another way to do this exercise. Place one hand on your lower abdomen, at least two finger-widths below your belly button, and focus on this area. It is enough to pay conscious attention to the fact that your abdomen is there, and you have found your center.

Your breathing doesn't get deeper:

Try the exercise the other way around: Center yourself first, and then move to "soft eyes." That should help with your breathing. It helps some individuals to change the order of the parts of this exercise—you may be able to feel something better, or it may make more sense to you.

You don't see what centering and "soft eyes" have to do with breathing:

Most people raise their chests too much when they are told to breathe deeply into the abdomen. That's not abdominal breathing. "Soft eyes" and centering are prerequisites for abdominal breathing. "Soft eyes" are necessary because a hard or fixed gaze usually does not allow you to breathe into your abdomen. And your center of gravity has to be at its lowest when your diaphragm is active, which only happens when you breathe into your abdomen. If you breathe shallowly, high in your chest, your center of gravity shifts slightly upwards—only a little, but enough to unbalance you more easily.

You don't see why "soft eyes" and centering are important:

Have you ever noticed how your eyesight and breathing change when you are afraid? When we feel we are in danger (whether real or imagined), we get tunnel vision (hard eyes), stress hormones are released, and we breathe more shallowly. Our heart rates and blood pressure also increase.

If you are able to consciously soften your gaze in a fearful situation and center yourself, the rest of the fear responses happening inside you will also ease to a certain degree. Moreover, only by employing soft eyes, deep breathing, and centering can you truly sit deeply in the saddle again. Remember, as soon as you stare or hold your breath, you have already given up your seat. So, if you continuously keep "soft eyes" and centering in mind and practice them, you will be better able to handle any unexpected movement of your horse. Your muscles will have an appropriate degree of tension, and you will be able to react more quickly to everything. When you are centered, you have more muscle power and, most importantly, it's significantly harder to knock you off balance.

So that you can soften your eyes at any time, center yourself from one second to the next, and automatically breathe deeper into the abdomen, it is essential to practice this process often—even if you don't actually need it, in the moment. We will combine this exercise with another element later so you remember to do it regularly.

Now, see how your ability to balance changes through centering, "soft eyes," and abdominal breathing. For this next exercise, you need a partner.

PROBLEMS AND SOLUTIONS

Feel free to watch the video for this.

>>> In this exercise, you'll need a partner to help determine the point at which you lose your balance. For this, you should agree on how you will signal to them that you are ready. I always tell my clients to nod slightly, because speaking can distract you too much.

>>> Stand facing each other and hold hands, with your arms extended but relaxed. Now find a spot on your partner's forehead and stare fixedly at that point. When you are concentrating and staring, nod to your partner, and try to stay in your place. Your partner will now gently and smoothly pull you forward, without jerking. See how much pulling from their side is necessary for you to lose your position.

>>> Try it again—but this time, you will look at the point on your partner's forehead with "soft eyes," letting your centering ball sink into your pelvis. When your gaze is soft and you are holding onto the image of the ball in your pelvis, nod to your partner, so that they gently pull you forward again.

>>> Did you feel a difference? Could you maintain your balance better? What did your partner feel when they pulled you?

>>> If you think it worked better the second time because you were prepared, do the exercise again with a hard gaze. Could you maintain your balance as well this time? It wouldn't surprise me if you couldn't.

https://equihypnosis.com/partnerexercise

Stand facing each other and hold hands.

Stare at your partner's forehead.

By the way, it's not a bad thing if the difference in your balance when using hard and soft eyes doesn't feel very significant to you at first. This exercise is also a matter of concentration and practice. But it's important to know that every time you fix your gaze, that sends a signal to your body that danger is lurking nearby. Your muscle tone increases, your breathing becomes shallower, and your pulse and blood pressure rise. Naturally, your horse feels these changes in you and becomes more tense and vigilant.

Many riders often stare at something—at their horses' ears, necks, or manes. By the time you notice you are doing this, you have already given up your seat and your ability to influence your horse efficiently. If your horse gets scared at such a moment and shies, you won't be able to compensate for this sudden movement as well as if you had had "soft eyes" and been centered. Your horse might not have shied at all, because your entire presence would have been calmer. Even if it is really the horse who is tense and vigilant, you are now at least able to positively affect the transmission of your own tension to him, to avoid making the situation worse.

With a rigid gaze, it's not easy to keep your balance.

Now let your gaze soften, and let the ball sink into your pelvis.

With a soft gaze, centered, it is quite easy to stay balanced.

>>> Soft Eyes and Centering—Partner Exercise

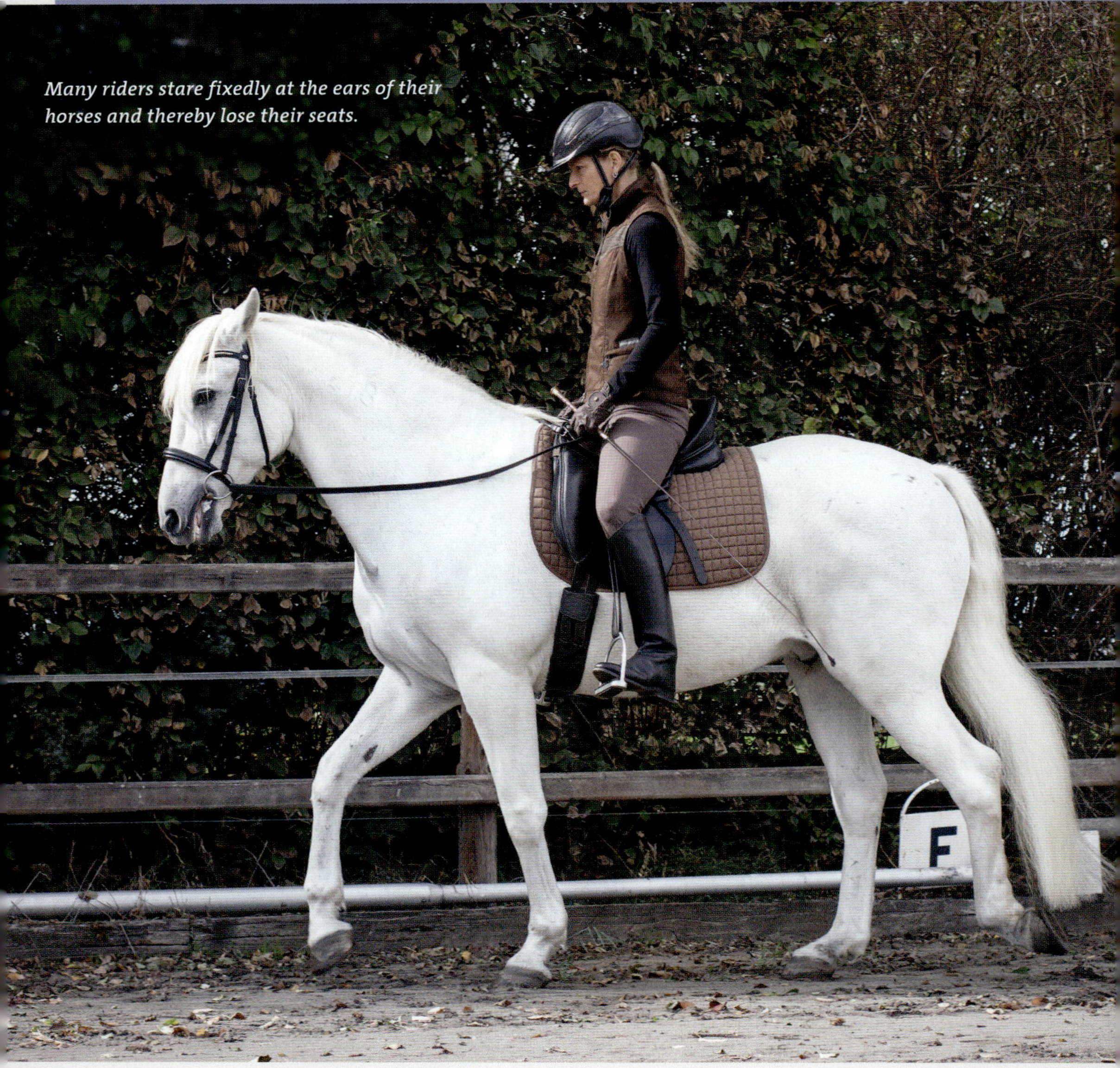

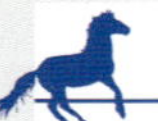

Many riders stare fixedly at the ears of their horses and thereby lose their seats.

TIP

Whenever you notice that you are staring hard at any one part of your horse or your surroundings, lift your head so you are looking straight ahead, then let your gaze soften and imagine the ball sinking into your pelvis.

If you are working with a coach or trainer, ask them to remind you about "soft eyes" and centering. They could ask you what your eyes are doing, or where the centering ball is. It's okay if you don't notice a big difference right away.

You can start this exercise at any time. Also, even when you aren't at the barn, you can still check whether your gaze is soft, what your breathing is like, and if you are centered, whenever you want.

How Mindfulness Can Help You

You're reading a book to overcome your fears, and now I'm approaching you with the idea of mindfulness. Strange, right? It's not that strange, actually, because being mindful in this context isn't about noticing dangers quickly. It's more about being truly mindful in the world around you, rather than getting lost in your own head. Because getting lost in your own head— your negative thoughts—is what you are doing when you indulge in your thought spirals about your fear. Mindfulness helps you stay in the moment, along with your horse. I have already discussed (on page 44) the fact that horses live more in the moment, and people usually don't. In that section, I also shared a Buddhist parable about living in the moment. When you are not mindful, you cannot fully connect with your horse.

If you can be entirely present in every moment, doing whatever you are doing, you will have little time to be afraid.

Perfect mindfulness is somewhat unrealistic when you're just beginning, of course, so we'll start smaller. Instead of engaging with your thoughts about your fear, which are oriented toward the future (after all, when you think about your fear, you are rarely thinking about what is happening right now, but rather what could happen at some future time), we will focus on your immediate reality. The best way to do this is by simply using your senses. Before I offer you an exercise for this, however, I want to remind you of something you may have already read or seen.

Are you familiar with the book *Momo* by Michael Ende, the author of *The Neverending Story*? In that book, there is an old street sweeper named Beppo, who explains to the main character, Momo, how to approach big tasks:

"You see, Momo," he told her one day, "it's like this. Sometimes, when you've a very long street ahead of you, you think how terribly long it is and feel sure you'll never get it swept... And then you start to hurry," he went on. "You work faster and faster, and every time you look up there seems to be just as much left to sweep as before, and you try even harder, and you panic, and in the end you're out of breath and have to stop—and the street stretches away in front of you. That's not the way to do it." He pondered a while. Then he said, "You must never think of the whole street at once, understand? You must only concentrate on the next step, the next breath, the next stroke of the broom... Nothing else... That way, you enjoy your work, which is important, because then you make a good job of it. And that's how it ought to be." There was another long silence. At last he went on, "And all at once, before you know it, you find you've swept the whole street clean, bit by bit. What's more, you aren't out of breath... That's important, too."

Beppo also explains that it creates fear when you deal too much with what lies ahead—when you spend all your time looking into the future. Instead, you should engage with what is present now. Since you don't have a street to sweep, I have a different task for you:

>>> Look around attentively, wherever you are right now, and mentally name five things you can see. It could sound something like this: "The lamp on the ceiling," "the yellow pillow," "the glass of water," "the picture on the wall," or "the plant."

>>> Now pay attention to the individual noises you can perceive. This is often difficult for us because we are used to filtering out many sounds that we hear frequently. Try it anyway, and name these sounds, too: "A passing car," "a bird chirping," "the ticking of the clock," "my breathing," "the creaking of a wooden floorboard."

>>> Now engage with the sense of touch; what can you feel at the boundary of your body or on your skin? "The shoes on my feet," "the ring on my finger," "a hair on my temple," "the waistband of my pants on my stomach when I breathe in," "the fabric of the sweater on my arms."

>>> Now also notice what you can currently smell and taste.

>>> Repeat the exercise with four things each, then three things, then two things, and finally with only one thing each, if the first round wasn't enough to completely focus you on reality.

After engaging intensively with your senses, you may find that you are not thinking about your fears anymore. In that case, you should not bring them back, but instead quietly continue to engage with the reality around you.

Likewise, when you are with your horse, focus entirely on what you are doing at the moment you are doing it. If you are grooming your horse, do it with all your attention. If it is difficult for you to stay focused, switch to using the brush or the curry comb with your other hand. Everything we do differently from usual requires more attention from us.

When was the last time you sat with your horse while he was eating his hay? Is there a more calming sound than that of a horse munching away? How often do you spend time with your horse while he does his favorite activities? Usually, we want something from our horses, and that's fine; but a truly sustainable relationship is created when both partners are important to each other, and they spend time together without needing to accomplish anything in particular.

Spending time together without any demand for performance.

Isn't that just distracting myself, or even suppressing my fear?

Contrary to what you might think, focusing on the present moment is not merely distraction from or suppression of your fears. You are focusing on what *is*, and on what you are doing, instead of on your fears. By the same token, if you do the opposite—if you focus on your fears and dwell on thoughts of the future—you let yourself be distracted from reality. Look at it this way: your fears are your distraction from reality, not the other way around. When you engage fully with reality, you are finally free of distractions. Suppression is different—it is a mechanism by which a topic or a thought is shifted from consciousness to the subconscious and kept under lock and key there. However, this repressed subject cannot be permanently held there; it will be released back into your consciousness at inopportune moments, because it takes a lot of energy for you to keep your subconscious suppressed.

What I suggest is this: face your fears, and work on them over the course of this book with self-hypnosis. You're not repressing anything, but rather ensuring that you can manage your everyday life without fear getting in your way. Also, the next time you are with your horse, be very mindful and attentive to both of you. Don't plan anything; just spend time with him. Enjoy his company. Here is an exercise to try.

>>> Walk very consciously to the pasture or paddock, when your horse is outside, and approach him slowly and mindfully. Only go as far as your horse would like you to—he will tell you.

>>> If he turns his hind end toward you, evades you in some way, or walks away, put some more distance between you two.

>>> If he turns toward you or his attention is with you, continue to approach carefully. If he comes toward you, all the better. Horses appreciate it when we just spend time with them without expecting anything.

>>> Stand next to your horse and breathe. Consciously perceive your surroundings. Stroke his coat and absorb the exact sensation of its texture on your palm, and against your fingertips.

>>> Just spend time there; observe your horse and the other horses in the group. Pay attention to the dynamics within the group. You might be able to recognize which horse has which role. (It is not always the horse that chases the others who is the highest in rank. Perhaps there is another horse everyone follows when he goes to the water or seeks another grassy spot in the pasture.)

>>> What small body signals do you notice that might have been hidden from you until now?

You can learn a lot by observing horses.

Are you a welcome visitor in your horse's pasture?

After becoming more aware of your surroundings and practicing more awareness in dealing with your horse, you can begin to proactively change your inner world, which is where your fear resides. The simplest and most effective method for this is hypnosis. That doesn't mean that you need someone else to hypnotize you—you can go far with self-hypnosis as well.

Self-hypnosis has many advantages. It is worth learning, and it is not difficult to do. Just follow me into the next section.

Self-Hypnosis

Self-hypnosis is a powerful tool you can use to find solutions for your personal problems, and to positively influence your thoughts, feelings, and behavior. The act of hypnosis is often misunderstood, so we will take a thorough look at what it entails. But before that, I would like to explain to you what hypnosis is.

BASICS OF SELF-HYPNOSIS

Hypnosis and self-hypnosis are used to make changes in a person while they are in a state of trance. The state of trance is used to make these changes because our brains are at their most pliable and adaptable in trance. In this state, new neuronal connections can form in the brain much more easily than they would normally.

Trance is actually a state of intense focus and high concentration. In this state, it is possible for us to find solutions we wouldn't come up with if we were fully conscious. In trance, we can delve into our subconscious minds, and have access to our unconscious feelings and memories.

Misunderstandings about Hypnosis

I find that many people view trance and hypnosis with skepticism and even fear. Often, this stems from a worry that you might not be able to wake up from a trance. If someone else is hypnotizing you, even more fears show up. Although we are dealing with self-hypnosis here, it is important to clear up some major misunderstandings about hypnosis in general.

Fear of Not Waking Up

The fear of remaining in a hypnotic trance would be understandable if it were a realistic possibility. But it actually isn't, because trance is a state that our brains create and dissolve within fractions of a second.

Believe it or not, we are in trance more than once every day, usually without realizing it, and yet no one gets stuck in it. Rather, our brains, on their own, restore conscious awareness, if the trance is not deliberately deepened further. If you are in trance and want to end this state, it is enough to intend to perceive your environment again and then open your eyes (if they were even closed). And that's exactly what you'll do. There is nothing that could stop you. If you want to get out of trance, it is possible at any time. Even if you wanted to stay in a state of trance, it wouldn't be possible over the long term, because your brain simply can't maintain this state permanently.

What Exactly Is Trance?

Trance is a completely normal state that your brain enters several times a day. It is a state of the highest concentration, where you are fully immersed in your world. You might have experienced something like this: You're driving your car, and are deep in thought about your day, revisiting some events. Maybe you wish you had acted differently in a particular situation, and mentally revisit this scenario. Then, suddenly, you become aware of your surroundings and quickly check the road in front of you for familiar landmarks to orient yourself. Maybe you ask yourself how you got there, because you can't really remember the last several minutes of the drive. Or you suddenly realize that you just missed your exit. This is a very typical example of an everyday trance, probably experienced by every driver at some point. Perhaps at other times, you have not noticed anything around you because you were engrossed in a book, a movie, or a computer game. In these moments, you were in trance.

Hypnosis is an ancient healing method that has been well researched in modern times. Today, we have a fairly good understanding of what happens in the brain during hypnosis. In fact, a significant research project was undertaken in Switzerland in the past few years in which 50 people were hypnotized while undergoing an MRI in order to explore what was happening in their brains in deep levels of trance.

Trance is fascinating because it allows access to our unconscious minds. Everything you have learned and experienced in your life, and then perhaps suppressed, is stored in your subconscious and can be brought to the surface during trance. Accessing the subconscious and communicating with it is significantly easier in trance than in a conscious state, which makes trance extremely effective for coaching and therapy. Moreover, our brains are at their most changeable in the state of trance, so any changes we want to make can be made more easily and have a greater likelihood of sticking. Our brains change throughout our lives as we learn and experience things, undergoing a perfectly natural, constant restructuring process. The technical term for this is neuroplasticity, and trance simply enhances this natural ability of the brain to change. And because our brains are so plastic and changeable, we can both learn and unlearn things. So if you have learned to feel fear while riding, there is no reason why you shouldn't be able to unlearn it.

A significant phase of restructuring in our brains occurs, for example, during puberty. If you have children who have already gone through or are currently going through this phase, you may have noticed changes when you are communicating with them during puberty. Things you taught them seem to be no longer retrievable. It is almost as if this knowledge never existed in their minds. This description might be a bit exaggerated, but drastic changes do happen in the brains of adolescents. Their thoughts, feelings, and behaviors change due to these alterations in their brains. Fortunately, this phase passes. However, to a certain extent, though not as drastically, this keeps happening throughout our lives.

Broadly speaking, the process of change in the brain can be described as follows: Neurons that are simultaneously active form a connection, creating a neuronal link. If this link is used regularly, it becomes stronger and faster, similar to our muscles when we exercise them. If the link is not used very much, it becomes slower and weaker. When it becomes obsolete, it is broken down and physically ceases to exist.

Let's return to trance. In trance, your perception is limited; you are focused on something specific, and everything else around you is relatively unimportant at that moment.

Myth: Not Everyone Can Be Hypnotized
There is a lot of misinformation and misunderstanding when it comes to each individual's ability to be hypnotized. Many people believe that someone with a "strong enough will" cannot be hypnotized, and that you need to be weak-willed to undergo hypnosis. This is a misconception. Hypnosis has little to do with willpower; it solely depends on how motivated you are to be hypnotized and to bring about a positive change in your situation.

In my experience, everyone whose brain can enter trance can be hypnotized. However, there are some precautions you should take if you suffer from epilepsy, cardiovascular disease, or psychosis. In these cases, you should certainly seek approval from your doctor.

If your doctor has no objections to you practicing, for instance, autogenic training or progressive muscle relaxation, then the kind of self-hypnosis you will learn here should be safe for you.

Why You Can Succeed with Hypnosis

You might still be doubting whether self-hypnosis is really for you, and whether you can actually hypnotize yourself. I know you can. I am absolutely sure of it. There will probably be moments when you are not sure if what you are experiencing is actually hypnosis, or days when it doesn't work very well. That's okay; everyone goes through this. Since trance is a state you are already familiar with and experience every day, self-hypnosis will probably not feel dramatic or unusual at first. Initially, the depth of your trance is not important. For our purposes, it's entirely sufficient if you are in a light trance.

Why do I know you can hypnotize yourself? Because I know you have a good imagination. After all, you are capable of imagining all sorts of terrifying scenarios happening to you while you are with your horse. It's the same for everyone who is dealing with a chronic fear: this strong imagination is both a blessing and a curse.

Fear Is Negative Self-Hypnosis

When you picture all the worst things could happen while you are riding your horse, you basically enter a trance. Thus, your fear is actually a kind of negative self-hypnosis. Every time you imagine a terrifying scenario, you are training your fear—and with every imagination session, your fear gets worse and appears more quickly. Essentially, you are causing the opposite of what you want to achieve. You might feel that you are dominated by these thoughts, but that doesn't have to be the case. You create your thoughts, and therefore you also have the power to change them. Going forward, you can use your strong imagination to your benefit to achieve your goals, because a good imagination is the most important thing you need for hypnosis and self-hypnosis. This is where the blessing lies.

What might be waiting for us during the ride?

Some Facts about Trance and Hypnosis

Most people have completely incorrect ideas about trance and hypnosis. A common stereotype is that hypnosis is fundamentally a state of relaxation. But relaxation is not hypnosis, nor is hypnosis the same as relaxation. In fact, trance also works in very tense

example of being in trance while driving), is proof that hypnosis is not fundamentally a relaxed state and can be performed with open eyes. Comparing trance to a conscious-awake state, the following differences are noticeable:

In a conscious-awake state, concentration and awareness are directed toward many different things, as we are almost always exposed to many changing stimuli. As a result, people are often somewhat scattered and not very focused. In trance, however, concentration and attention are directed inward. Perception shifts; external stimuli such as noises or tactile sensations are only superficially perceived, not perceived at all, or only accorded minor significance. When in trance, your consciousness focuses on internal processes.

Whenever perception and concentration shift from outside to inside, trances also occur. There are different degrees of immersion into these inner experiences, which are sometimes interpreted as different trance depths.

Trance is something continuous, on the one hand, but something flowing, too, on the other, so very different experiences and behaviors can emerge in hypnotized individuals. Though it gets used often, "trance depth" is not actually a well-chosen term, as we often think it means we should experience more intense feelings the deeper we are in trance. This is untrue, especially when you are just beginning to learn how to perform self-hypnosis. The more practiced we are with self-hypnosis, the more intense trance can feel.

states, such as after an accident or in a frightening situation. Another misconception is that your eyes must be closed during hypnosis. You definitely don't need closed eyes for hypnosis or trance. In fact, active-awake hypnosis, where you engage in physical activity with your eyes open (such as in our previous

Even if you often go into trance, it is important to practice safe self-hypnosis techniques, which means the experience may at first be pretty mild. Eventually, over time, it will likely feel more intense.

There are several indicators of trance that you may experience:

- Enhanced swallowing reflex
- Fluttering of the eyelids (easily visible in the eye-lashes)
- With open eyes: dilated pupils; fixed, possibly blurred gaze
- REM movements, staring, or scanning movements of the pupils
- Reddened areas on the neck and upper chest
- Slack facial features
- Relaxed superficial muscles
- Change in skin color
- Tilting of the head
- Decreased skin conductance
- Change in resting pulse rate
- Urge to laugh
- Soft and monotonous voice
- Robotic movements
- Ideomotor reactions (spontaneous movements of your body or body parts)
- Toes tilting outward while lying on your back
- Spontaneous muscle twitching
- Stomach/intestinal noises
- The feeling of falling asleep

These signs don't all appear simultaneously, and you won't necessarily experience all of them. You may feel either a physical heaviness or lightness. You might wonder how much time has passed. Notably, it is easiest to recognize trance after it is over, especially when you first start practicing self-hypnosis. When we return to the here and now, we usually notice a slight change in state, similar to when we notice while driving that we were preoccupied with our thoughts. This realization is essentially waking up from trance, and it feels similar when we've just been in a state of self-hypnosis.

The more often you practice self-hypnosis, the deeper trance can become, and the more intensely you might experience it. However, it is not necessary to achieve deep and intense trance states to resolve fear or other issues.

If you want, listen to one of the hypnosis MP3s ("Source of Power" or "Mastering Situations"); then you'll have a better idea of how the process goes. I would recommend the hypnosis MP3 "Source of Power" for this.

Source of Power
Duration: 24 Minutes

This MP3 is a guided trance or hypnosis. It lasts about 24 minutes. I will start speaking after one minute. This gives you enough time to get comfortable and turn off your mobile phone. Lie down, or sit comfortably. It's absolutely okay if you fall asleep during this, as your subconscious continues to absorb things even when you are no longer consciously listening to what is being said.

Please do not listen to this MP3 while driving!

https://equihypnosis.com/source

Is there a more hypnotic sound than horses chewing hay?

You should be aware that self-hypnosis often feels less intense than when you are hypnotized by another person. Many people who learn self-hypnosis often wonder if what they are feeling is how it ought to feel, and that's normal. If you have already listened to one of the MP3s in this book, that's a good reference point for what it could feel like for you.

What You Should Also Know

You can't do much wrong in self-hypnosis. It's normal if your thoughts drift, or if you wonder whether you are doing everything right. That's okay. It might confuse you that your consciousness is still active and you can think, rather than closing out all that external "noise." But you need your ability to think consciously in order to practice self-hypnosis, because you have to be able to think about what the next step is.

Initiating Self-Hypnosis

There are numerous ways to induce trance in yourself, and I would like to explain three different options to you. You can try each one separately to see what works best for you. To better understand what this should look like, watch the videos for each one. Eventually, you may also combine all the introductory self-hypnosis exercises with each other and apply them one after another in a way that feels good for you.

First, read through all three options completely—both the technique and the completion of (or exit from) trance. It's important that you only try one of these variants after you have read the exit instructions. The exercises for this will follow in the next few sections.

a) Pika-Pika Breathing

View hypnos
inductions a:
emergence
with video, c
listen to the

>>> This breathing technique quickly brings you into trance. It reduces pain and anxiety.

>>> Imagine while inhaling that the fresh air is flowing through the top of your skull and into your body.

>>> Imagine while exhaling that the used air is flowing out of the soles of your feet.

>>> Stay focused on this for several minutes.

Inhale through the crown of your head and exhale through the soles of your feet.

(video of all techniques)

https://equihypnosis.com/selfhypnosis

https://equihypnosis.com/pikapika

>>> Close your eyes, take a deep breath, and exhale.

>>> Notice all the individual sounds you can hear; each sound helps you focus on yourself.

>>> Focus on your breathing without changing it.

>>> Mentally count from one to ten, while imagining yourself going down something.

What you imagine yourself going down is entirely up to you. It can be a staircase, an escalator, or just a path that runs a bit downhill. You can also imagine sliding down a playground slide or water slide. It really doesn't matter what you imagine. It also doesn't matter how you imagine it—whether you see it with your inner eye or focus on the sensation of going downward. It's okay if you initially can't decide whether it's a clear or blurry image, or whether you are experiencing it from the inside or seeing it from the outside.

The most important thing is that you have the impression of going downward while counting.

Walk down something mentally—maybe this path?

https://equihypnosis.com/goingdownsomething

c) Palm Line Induction

>>> Extend an arm with the palm of your hand facing you. Focus on the lines of your palm.

>>> Next, while maintaining a fixed gaze, slowly bring your palm toward your face. As soon as your hand touches your face, close your eyes and let your arm fall—as if your arm were like overcooked spaghetti.

Focus your gaze on the lines of your palm.

Allow your hand to sink toward your face.

This induction is particularly effective if you assure yourself beforehand that your subconscious will lead you to the optimal trance depth as soon as your hand touches your face.

https://equihypnosis.com/handline

You will go into a trance as soon as your eyes close and your arm falls.

EXITING SELF-HYPNOSIS

To come back to conscious awareness from trance (emergence), there are also many options. I will introduce only three of these, all of which you are welcome to try.

a) At Your Own Pace

>>> Plan to be back here and now immediately.

>>> Take another deep breath; move your fingers, feel the surface on which you are sitting or lying, hear the sounds in your environment, and open your eyes.

b) Going Up Something

This emergence technique is particularly suitable if you imagined going down something to enter trance.

Plan to return to everyday consciousness immediately.

>>> Imagine now that you are going up something while counting to ten.

>>> When you have reached the top or 10, take a deep breath; move your fingers, hands, and feet; become aware of your environment again; and open your eyes.

c) Counting Yourself Out

You can also use this emergence technique in addition to one of the others, if you don't feel one hundred percent consciously awake after you have used another technique.

>>> **Say to yourself: I will count to three shortly, and when I reach three, I will open my eyes and be back here and now, completely awake. 1, 2, 3—open your eyes!**

Exercise: Induction into and Emergence from Trance

Choose induction and emergence techniques that you want to try. I would suggest you first bring yourself into trance with "Going Down Something," and then use "Going Up Something" to emerge from it.

>>> **Read both again, and then just do it.**

>>> **Try the other methods afterward.**

PROBLEMS AND SOLUTIONS

You don't feel like you're fully consciously awake again.

If you do not feel completely, consciously awake after the trance, you can close your eyes again and count yourself out.

Rest assured the trance will also dissolve on its own eventually if it is not deliberately deepened further, because our brains do not want to constantly maintain this state. Basically, it is enough to just wait, and after thirty to forty-five minutes at most, the feeling will have vanished. If you don't want to wait that long, eat and drink a little something and go outside for a moment. That should be enough to get you into a more consciously awake state.

You feel a bit dizzy, or you have a headache.

If you feel a bit dizzy or headachy after your trance, it is likely because you came out of trance too quickly. Just close your eyes again, take a few deep breaths, and return to the here and now at your own pace. Take your time feeling the sensations in your body, as well as the surface on which you are sitting or lying. Plan to be completely consciously awake in the next moment. Move your fingers, hands, and feet; take another deep breath; and then open your eyes.

In this case, too, these symptoms will disappear by themselves after a little while. Nevertheless, you can count yourself out as described in the previous solution, eat and drink a little something, and then go outside for a moment to get some fresh air.

You're not sure if you were in trance or if you were deep enough in trance.

Doubting whether your trance was deep enough is quite normal at first; we usually expect trance to feel very different from our usual state. However, because it is a normal state that you probably experience several times a day, experiencing it through self-hypnosis won't necessarily give you a totally unfamiliar feeling. Plus, you probably only spent a short moment in trance the first time, which rarely feels significantly different from simply closing your eyes and relaxing a bit. Also, as discussed above, the idea of trance "depth" is not useful, because we associate that term with intensity of feeling in a way that leads us to expect greater intensity with increased depth. Initially, that probably won't be the case for you. Trance intensity comes with practice, so the more often we practice self-hypnosis, the more intense it can eventually feel. I won't discuss trance depths or levels further here, because for our purposes, it is irrelevant whether you are in light, medium, or deep trance.

To determine if you were in trance, you can refer to the list of signs on page 76. Or you can try to perceive how you felt while listening to the "Source of Power" MP3. When you came out of trance, did it feel a little like when you suddenly become aware of your surroundings when you have gotten lost in thought while driving? Then you were definitely in trance. If you're still unsure, ignore this question for now and continue with the exercises anyway. You will be able to feel it better each time. Remember, we already know you enter trance easily, because of the fact that you have fears. Once you accept that, it is very likely that you will also go into trance during these exercises. Also, feel free to try combining the hypnosis inductions with each other to see if that helps you enter trance more easily. Another aid for you are the videos, which show you what it looks like when someone who does this very often goes into trance.

The Safe Place

This exercise will be the focal point of your continuing journey. The opposite of the feeling of fear is the feeling of ease and safety, so we are going to create a safe place for you where you will feel at ease. We want to evoke feelings of security and safety in you, and strengthen them. The safe place is ideal for this—you can go there mentally whenever you need to, after you have created it. Later on, you may not even have to go into trance, because it will happen automatically when you enter your safe place.

The safe place is a mental place in your imagination. It doesn't have to physically exist, though most of my clients initially use a place that is well known to them, such as their own bed or their living room couch. That's fine, if you really feel safe there and it's a place where no one else intrudes on you. If that's not the case, though, change your safe place. If you find that the place you have thought of isn't working well, you can change it at any time.

A safe place by a tree.

Self-Hypnosis: Safe Place

You can also listen to the instructions for setting up a safe place as an MP3..

>>> Put yourself in trance, and then imagine a place where you feel absolutely safe. It can be a place you know, one you may have seen before, or one you dream up out of thin air. It can be a very simple place, like a couch or under a blanket, or a place that only exists in your imagination—for example, on a cloud, deep down in the sea, or on another planet. Anything is possible.

The important thing is that you feel truly comfortable and safe there. You can customize this place so it is exactly what you want. If it is a place in nature, you can imagine it as wide open, or give it boundaries if that makes it feel safer. It's your choice.

>>> This place is there only for you. You alone are the ruler of this place, and you alone determine whether anyone gets access or not.

https://equihypnosis.com/safeplace

It is your place. You can withdraw mentally there at any time to rest and recharge. This place is made so you are absolutely safe and protected. If you want to make any modifications so it is even safer and more comfortable, you can do that at any time. Make note of the following things:

>>> Where is your place? Is it outside or inside?

>>> Are you sitting, standing, or lying down?

>>> Where are you looking?

>>> What surrounds you?

>>> How do you feel there?

>>> Where can you sense this feeling in your body?

>>> If this feeling had a color, what color would it be?

>>> What makes you feel that way there?

>>> Be very aware of the feeling and its color.

>>> Imagine your safe feeling surrounding you, as if it fills the atmosphere in your safe place, as if it is in the air and you can breathe it in. With each breath you take, you absorb this feeling into yourself. It's almost as if the air is imbued with the feeling's color, and as if you are breathing in this hue.

>>> Imagine it flowing into your lungs, into your heart, and being distributed throughout your body from there. It flows into your entire chest, into your stomach, and into your pelvis.

>>> Imagine this colored feeling flowing into your legs, into your feet, and even into your toes. With each breath you take, it becomes stronger and fills you up more fully. It flows into your shoulders, into your arms, into your hands, and into your fingers and the tips of your toes. With each breath, this good feeling fills you until you glow and shine from the inside with this color.

>>> Imagine also that in your safe place there is a very special light that envelops you, as if you were surrounded by a sphere or bubble of light, like a protective shell. This light gives you protection and security; nothing that could harm you can pass through the light. It is absolutely impermeable to anything harmful. This light surrounds you with protection and security.

>>> What's special about this light is that it can flow into you. You can breathe it in, and it can also sink into you through your skin, like sunlight.

>>> Imagine that this light no longer just surrounds you, but also flows into you, and you are breathing it in.

>>> Imagine that this light can flow into every one of your cells, and that everywhere it flows, it brings protection and security. Every cell can be bathed in this light and recharge. You may find that there are parts of your body that particularly need a lot of this light. If so, that's absolutely fine, because you will never run out of light—the light is infinite, and can keep flowing forever. Every cell is renewed by this light, bringing protection and security and facilitating healing. The light flows into every cell and surrounds you. It flows into every corner of your mind and soul. Everywhere it goes, it brings protection and security. The light completely envelops and fills you, ensuring that the good feeling inside you becomes strong and powerful.

>>> Here in your safe place, surrounded by the light, you are absolutely safe and protected. Nothing can harm you.

>>> Enjoy your place, the light, and the feeling, and deeply absorb it.

>>> When you are ready, breathe in the light and the feeling deeply once again, and take it with you as you gradually return to the here and now. Guide yourself out of the trance.

Notes

It's best to write down what your safe place looks like. If you like, paint or draw it, and make it as real as possible for yourself. Write down how you feel there, and what color the feeling of safety and the light have.

Spend some mental time there every day to enhance the effect. Remember, it's okay if your safe place changes, as long as you feel comfortable and safe there.

You can't find a safe place.

If you can't immediately find or imagine a safe place, you need to figure out why this is the case. Is it because you actually can't find a safe place, or is it because you can't make up your mind? That's okay. Gradually it will become clear to you where you can truly feel comfortable and safe, even if you don't recognize it right away. For now, you can simply pick a place you think might work and try other places at a later time. If you simply can't think of a suitable place right now, how about the meadow from the "Source of Power" MP3? Do you feel comfortable and safe there? Give it a try and see.

Sometimes a person can't find a safe place because they can't imagine feeling perfectly safe anywhere. Does this trigger you? If so, sometimes it works well to just imagine the light around you, without creating a safe space first. However, if this topic triggers you overall, you might want to consider trauma therapy or, if you are already in therapy, consult your therapist. Furthermore, mindfulness exercises are very important for you; you should do them regularly.

The light doesn't flow everywhere.

If you feel as though the light can't flow everywhere in your body, then there is a blockage—and you can resolve it. Imagine that not only are you breathing in the light, but it is also sinking through your skin and into your body. You can also imagine that the light is drawn specifically to places where it doesn't flow, as if attracted there by a magnet. The concentration of light there can help dissolve the blockage. It's entirely up to you how you get things moving, because it's your imagination and you can change it at any time. Imagine whatever makes the most sense to you to solve this problem.

You might decide you feel safe in the horse pasture.

Evoking And Integrating Secure Feelings

It is easiest to communicate directly with your subconscious and access unconscious thoughts and feelings when you are in a trance. Therefore, having easy access to your safe place and feelings is important for your journey. This way, you can make a feeling of security more consistently present in yourself, so you can access it more easily later.

Your secure moment is in your past. It could have been a moment with or without a horse.

You can also listen to this part as an MP3.

>>> Enter into trance and then continue into your safe place, which you should know and have established well by now.

>>> Imagine the light around and within you, giving you protection and security. Focus on your feelings and the body perceptions that you have in this place. Mentally review the following: Do you feel safe there? What does it feel like there? Where can you perceive this safe feeling in your body? How would you describe how you feel in your safe place? If this feeling had a color, what color would it be? Focus entirely on this feeling inside you and on this color, while you continue to be mentally enveloped and filled with the light in your safe place.

>>> This secure or good feeling inside you connects you to all the moments in which you have ever felt this way. Focus on your feeling of safety, and mentally count to three. When you reach 3, or perhaps even earlier, a situation in which you felt good and safe will come to mind. It may be like a memory, or you might almost feel like you are experiencing it all over again.

>>> Count to three: 1—2—3. You are now in a moment where you feel really good and safe. Are you indoors or outdoors in this moment? Is it light or dark? Are you alone, or is someone with you?

>>> What is happening in this moment? How do you feel? Where in your body can you perceive this feeling? If it had a color, what color would it be? What makes you feel this way? Is there anything else there that is important to you?

https://equihypnosis.com/securemoment

>>> Imagine that this feeling and its associated color exist all around you, so you can breathe them in.

>>> Imagine breathing them in deeply. They flow into your lungs, into your heart, and spread throughout your body from there. They flow into your chest and your stomach. They flow into your pelvis, into your legs, down to your feet, and even into your toes. And they continue to spread within you, with every breath. They flow into your shoulders, your arms, down to your hands and fingertips. And still further with each breath, into your neck and head, until you are completely filled with this feeling and your color—until you shine and radiate from within in this color.

>>> Take another deep breath of this feeling and absorb the atmosphere of this moment fully within you; then return to your safe place, taking the feeling and color with you. There, the feeling becomes part of the light, so that every time you are mentally in your safe place and that light surrounds and fills you, you will also be filled with this feeling and can recharge with it.

>>> If you want, you can continue directly into the next exercise now.

REMOVING BLOCKAGES

The removal of blockages is a very effective hypno-therapeutic intervention that is often used because it can facilitate significant change. It also works wonderfully in self-hypnosis. Through the removal of blockages, it is possible to let go of the old and free yourself from obstacles that prevent you from doing what you want. The removal of blockages is often formulated in general terms, which allows the subconscious to decide what can be let go. Possibly, more blockages will be released than you thought, and issues or problems that you didn't even consider may disappear. Naturally, you always have your fear in mind, and your subconscious knows what you want to change, so it will also address your fear.

The removal of blockages can have a profound impact, and doing it once might be enough. It is also a good way to free yourself later from other accumulated issues that may not be related to your fear—for example, if you are having a difficult time with your job.

>>> Your starting point is your safe place and the light, as soon as you are in trance.

>>> Now imagine there is a beautiful waterfall near you. You can hear it and you walk toward it. When you reach it, you see that the water sparkles in the sun, and when you stretch out your hand, you feel that the water is pleasantly warm and gentle. It is very special water that can cleanse you from everything you have been carrying around for far too long.

>>> The waterfall is at a comfortable height for you and is wide enough for you to stand under.

>>> So you now stand under the warm, soft, flowing water, while your subconscious takes the opportunity to let go of everything holding you back, everything that is preventing you from being who you want to be. Your subconscious knows precisely what it can let go of.

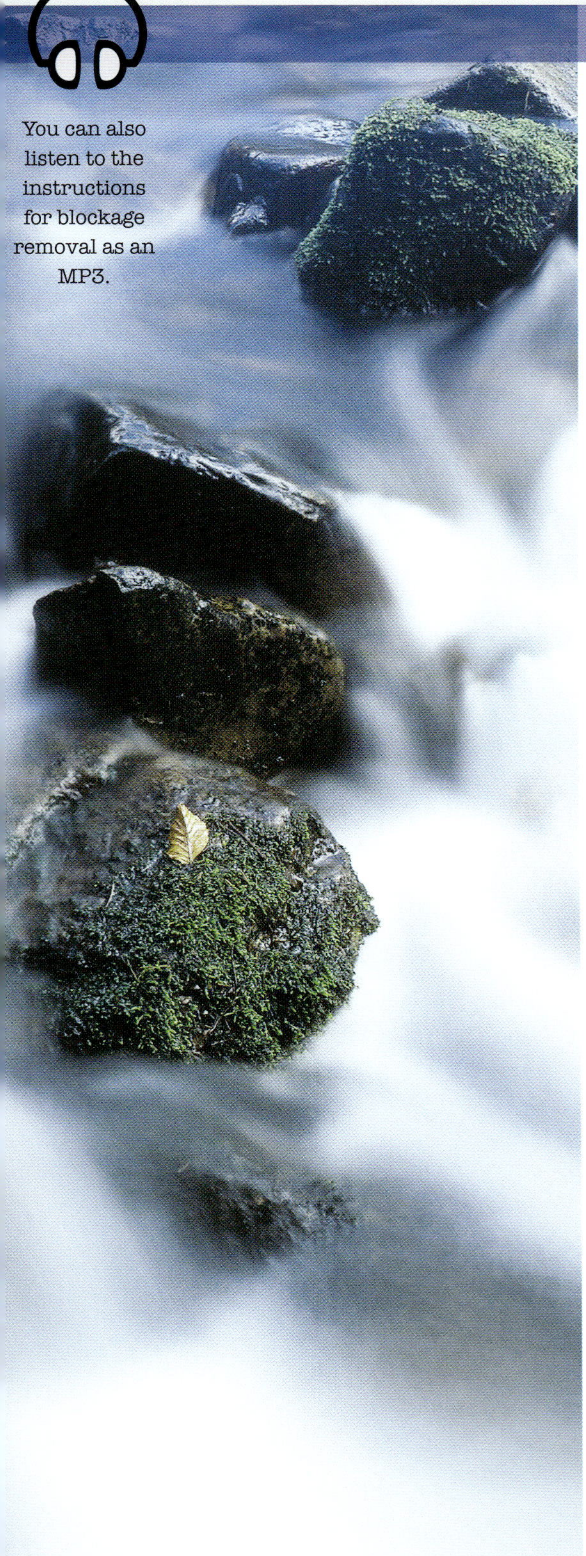

https://equihypnosis.com/removal

>>> It looks into every corner of you and does a kind of spring cleaning. You might remember moments that made you the way you are now, but that's not necessary. You can now let all that go, and the water washes it away. The water removes everything that you've carried in your heart, body, mind, and soul that has been preventing you from being free for too long, and carries it away. It flows away from you, very far away, so that it has no influence on you. Sometimes the things being washed and carried away are small things that, surprisingly, have become a problem for the subconscious. Sometimes they are things from childhood, adolescence, or adult life. Maybe they are incidents with people. Regardless, your subconscious sorts out what it can let go of, and everything is washed away by the water. You might feel it flowing out of you like a gentle, quiet stream, or you might feel lighter, or maybe you visualize it flowing away. It really doesn't matter. Your subconscious knows exactly what it can let go of and now takes the opportunity to do so.

>>> The water takes everything with it that can be let go of, everything that is holding you back from being happy and doing what you want to do; the subconscious lets go of it and it is carried away by the water.

>>> It flows farther and farther away from you. It has no further influence over you.

>>> Now, go back to the light that envelops and fills you. It gives you protection and security. Maybe you can already feel today that your subconscious has less to deal with, and much more energy to support you in achieving your goals. Over the next days and nights, it will rearrange everything inside you, so that every day, in every way, you feel better and better. The light is still around you, flowing into you, containing everything you need to be well and achieve what you want.

>>> Enjoy the light and breathe it in deeply. Recharge yourself with it; then take it with you and exit trance.

I Shape My Future In Trance

After you have evoked and anchored secure feelings within yourself and have also let go of blockages, it is now possible to envision your future in trance.

Future vision: having fun cantering in an open field.

Exercise: Future Vision

The starting point for this exercise is again your safe place in trance. The light, which gives you protection and security, is around you and fills you up. You are absolutely safe and protected there.

>>> In a moment, you will mentally count to three. When you reach three, you will be in a situation in your future where you feel really comfortable and good. At three, or maybe sooner, you will be in your future at a moment when your fears are already behind you and you have accomplished what you wish for. At three or sooner, you will be in a moment with your horse where you feel good and truly comfortable.

>>> Now count to three: 1—2—3. You are in a moment where you feel really good and secure, where your problem is already behind you—a moment with your horse. Are you indoors or outdoors in this moment? Is it light or dark? Are you alone, or is someone with you?

>>> What is happening right now? How do you feel? Where in your body do you perceive this feeling? If the feeling had a color, what color would it be? What causes you to feel this way at this moment? If you are riding at the moment, how does your horse feel beneath you?

>>> Is there anything else important to you right now?

>>> Imagine that this feeling and its corresponding color are all around you, so you can breathe it in. It's as if you are riding in a cloud of this feeling and this color—a cloud that envelops you and your horse.

>>> Imagine breathing it in deeply. It flows into your lungs, into your heart, and spreads throughout your body from there. It flows into your chest and into your abdomen. It flows into your pelvis, into your legs, down to your feet, and even into the tips of your toes. And it still continues to spread within you with every breath. It flows into your shoulders, into your arms, down to your hands and fingertips. And it continues further with every breath, into your neck and head, until you are entirely filled with this feeling and your color—until you glow and radiate from within in this color.

You can also listen to the instructions for establishing a vision of your future as an MP3.

In your safe place, there is a very special light.

>>> Take a deep breath of this feeling once again, and deeply absorb the atmosphere of this moment. If you could take a symbol of this moment back to your safe place, what would it be? You could, for example, imagine taking a photo of this moment and framing it, so you can take it to your safe place, put it there, and look at it anytime.

>>> Then, go back to your safe place, and take the feeling and the color of this moment there. In that place, it will become part of the light, so that every time you mentally are in your safe place and the light surrounds and fills you, you are also filled with this feeling, and it can recharge you. There, you can also remember this moment in your future.

>>> If you have taken a picture of it, you can look at it anytime in your safe place. Your subconscious will be attracted to this moment like a powerful magnet, and it will align everything inside you so that it comes true.

>>> Every day, in every way, you feel better and better.

https://equihypnosis.com/vision

SELF-HYPNOSIS IN EVERYDAY LIFE

Suggestions in Self-Hypnosis

Suggestions constantly affect us. Even if we are not aware of it, we continuously program ourselves with our suggestions. Often, these are negative, meaning we sabotage ourselves.

As long as you see yourself as overweight, for instance, you remain overweight, because your brain tries to maintain the status quo. That is why it is useful to replace negative suggestions with positive ones.

The most effective suggestions are linked with feelings and other sensory perceptions. In the case of fear, this happens automatically. I would now like to explain how you can create beneficial suggestions for yourself, which you can combine with other self-hypnosis exercises.

How should suggestions be structured?

Positive suggestions are conscious, goal-oriented, focus on the desired result, and do not include any difficulties—for example, "Every time I ride my horse, I am calm, relaxed, and focused." Positive, active suggestions meet these six criteria:

1. Phrased positively

It is essential to phrase a suggestion positively. So, instead of "I am not afraid," say, "I am calm and focused." I would also avoid terms like "fearless," because our brains struggle with negations. Instead, use terms that describe what you want to replace your fear with. Do you want to ride out with relaxation? Enjoy a calm canter? Jump with joy?

2. Simple—one sentence

People often tend to use complex sentences when it comes to their wishes. They want to consider all eventualities or explain their desires. Instead, simply state what you desire, not why.

3. Credible

A suggestion is only useful if it is believable to you. Anything you can't believe is rejected by your subconscious and has no effect. If you can't imagine galloping across a stubble field someday, then choose another suggestion. For instance, you can proceed more incrementally; focus your suggestion on simply cantering the long side of the outdoor arena. You might also want to reflect on what came to you in the future vision exercise. What words could underline those images, perceptions, and feelings?

4. Measurable

You should be able to tell whether your suggestion has been effective or not. So you need some standard you can use to measure change. This can be as simple as an adjective you can recognize when it appears. For instance, if you wish to experience a relaxed ride and choose "relaxed" as part of your suggestion, if you have not been able to remember what a relaxed ride might feel like, you will surely notice when you find yourself thinking a ride feels "relaxed" to you.

5. In the present

It is essential to phrase your suggestions in the present, as if they are already a reality. So, not, "I will be relaxed at the trot," but "I am relaxed at the trot."

6. Rewarding

The suggestion should be rewarding to achieve. You want to feel good about it—"I am relaxed at the trot and feel good."

Here is a simple example of a suggestion that includes all the above-mentioned criteria: "Every morning at 7 o'clock, I ride a bicycle for 20 minutes, and I feel healthy and strong."

>>> Write a positive suggestion on a personal issue that you want to change. Use a single simple sentence, not complex sentences. The suggestion should include your goal and, above all, no difficulties.

>>> Check whether it meets the six criteria:
1. Phrased positively
2. Simple—one sentence
3. Credible
4. Measurable
5. In the present
6. Rewarding

>>> Practice daily self-hypnosis, go to your safe place, and tell yourself your suggestion. You are welcome to repeat it a few times.

>>> A suggestion works even better if you imagine a situation in which you have already achieved what is outlined in your suggestion. It might be your vision of the future, or it might be something else. Finally, imagine the light that includes everything and gives you protection and security. Breathe it in deeply once more before leaving trance.

Always remember the basics.

Tips and Tricks

It is important that you practice self-hypnosis as often as possible in the next few days and weeks, ideally daily. See how you can best incorporate it into your daily routine, and understand that it's normal for it to work better on some days and less well on others. You can perform self-hypnosis while standing, lying down, or sitting (though doing it while standing can be somewhat uncomfortable over time). Stay in that state as long as you can maintain the visualizations. If you notice that you are, for example, thinking instead about something you still need to buy, then mentally return to your safe place and the light, and then exit trance. It's not essential to extend the duration of the self-hypnosis, and it's pointless if your thoughts are already elsewhere. Let it be good for the moment; tomorrow is another, better day.

You can perform self-hypnosis at whatever time of the day suits you. You don't need much time for it.

However, if you have plans afterward or are afraid of falling asleep, it would be better to set an alarm or other notification. It's okay if you fall asleep during self-hypnosis, by the way, so you can absolutely practice self-hypnosis in bed before sleeping (though if you regularly fall asleep during the initiation of hypnosis, it's better to find another place or time of day).

A typical characteristic of trance is that we lose our sense of time while we are in it. Usually, we underestimate the time we spend in trance compared to the actual time (in other words, it feels like you've been in trance for only a couple minutes, but in reality it's been more like 20 minutes). The opposite is also possible, but happens less often.

On days when you feel you can't concentrate on anything, listen to the MP3 "Mastering Situations." Listening works better on such days than trying to focus on self-hypnosis.

You always fall asleep during self-hypnosis.

If you have tried self-hypnosis sitting and lying down at different times of the day, but fall asleep every time, your body apparently needs to catch up on sleep. Since you need your consciousness for self-hypnosis, you don't benefit much if you fall asleep, because then your conscious mind also sleeps. In this case, listen to the MP3 "Mastering Situations" instead. Your subconscious listens even if you are asleep, so you can fall asleep while listening.

You can't engage in self-hypnosis lately.

When we are in a stressful phase, overwhelmed at work, or having problems in a relationship, it's often not easy to focus. We quickly get distracted by our problems and feel like we can't enter trance. Especially in times when we need self-hypnosis the most, it's often not easy to stay on track. For that, we would have to ignore our feeling of not being able to engage and still practice self-hypnosis. The more practiced you are, the easier it will be, but if you are still just starting out with self-hypnosis, it can be very frustrating. In these cases, listen to the MP3 "Mastering Situations" instead, even if this phase lasts for a while. Listen to it until you can practice self-hypnosis again. I actually have some clients who only listen to that MP3, because they find it more pleasant. That's okay, even though I always recommend that you practice self-hypnosis again. That way, when you need it, you are still somewhat practiced.

Another problem has appeared.

Sometimes we have basically solved a problem and suddenly a new, more urgent problem appears. In this case, focus on the most important problem at the moment.

You can use all the exercises for self-hypnosis for this problem. Continue to use your safe place, and work on this new problem by removing blockages and working with suggestions. If the problem resolves, return to your original fear of riding, if that fear still exists.

Continue to use your soft gaze, the ball, and the safe place while riding. In general, all the techniques you now know can be used to work on any problem.

https://equihypnosis.com/masteringsituations

The movements of your horse can easily bring you into trance.

SELF-HYPNOSIS WHILE RIDING

Eventually, when you are centered and have a soft gaze while on your horse, you will be able to enter trance quite easily. The rhythmic movements of your horse, combined with your imagination, will help with this. You have learned about your safe place and the light that gives you protection and security. When you combine all of this while on your horse, not only will your feelings change, your seat will also. Going forward, when I speak about the basics, I'm referring to a soft gaze, breathing, the ball, the safe place, and the light.

You don't specifically need to initiate hypnosis on the horse because, as mentioned, you can quickly enter trance while riding. Many people think it is dangerous to go into hypnosis while riding, but the opposite is true.

You don't close your eyes when initiating trance while riding; you use the basics for centered riding. You use soft eyes to look where you want to ride, you breathe to your center, and you think about the ball centering you in your pelvis. Then you imagine you are in your safe place. The light is around you and within you, giving you protection and security. Imagine riding in a cloud of colored light, and the light also surrounds your horse, so both of you are completely enveloped in it. You will feel much more connected to your horse, and since you are completely balanced within yourself, your horse will also pay careful attention to you. When you are in trance, you don't have to focus intently on your aids or pay close attention to your seat, because when you are in your safe place and the light and you feel good, your muscles will, as if by magic, perform the way you want them to.

Imagine you both are enveloped by your colored cloud of light.

Your subconscious is your protection mechanism, which is why we react more quickly when we are in trance. Because you are riding centered and with a soft gaze, you are optimally balanced, too. Through imagining your safe place and the calm and security you feel there, you can sit more deeply in the saddle and influence your horse more easily. Overall, you need to employ significantly less effort than when fully conscious.

When you begin to use these exercises to return to confident riding, it is initially helpful to practice self-hypnosis before you ride, especially if you want to face what has scared you up until now. So, if you have planned to undertake a first ride out again, you should do self-hypnosis before you go to the stable. Always mentally go to your safe place with the light as soon as you think about riding out. Also, incorporate a soft gaze and the ball. Recall these thoughts while preparing your horse, before you mount, and as soon as you are on the horse, too.

You can also do self-hypnosis on the horse.

Remember the basics: soft gaze, centering, safe place, and light.

The basics are important while mounting, too.

Also, keep the basics in mind while you are on the horse.

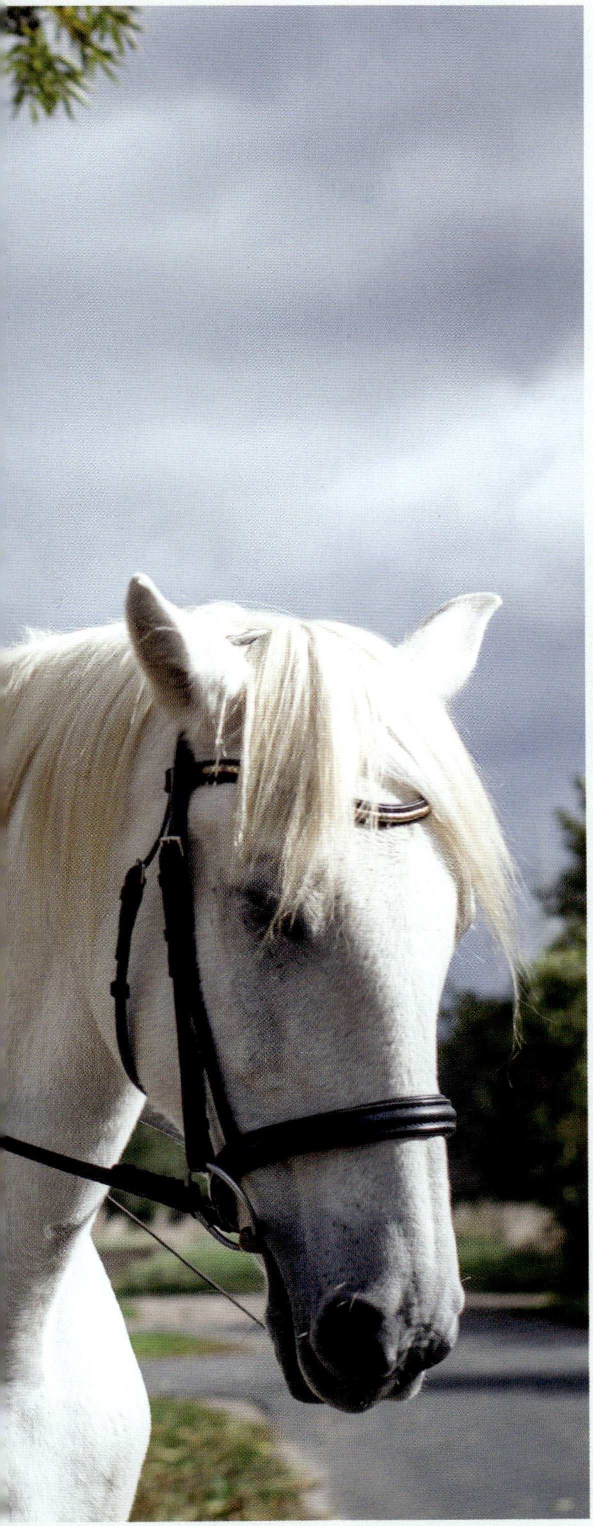

TIPS & TRICKS

Once you've gotten reasonably comfortable at a walk, you can prepare yourself for anything new or anything that seems difficult to you by using your imagination, soft gaze, and the ball concept.

As you return to riding, approach everything step by step and make it as simple as possible. If you feel more comfortable doing so, it's perfectly fine to find someone you trust to help you for now. This person can guide you so you can focus entirely on yourself, and you don't have to drive or steer while engaging in self-hypnosis. Later, when it comes to faster gaits, this person can work with you on a longe line, or they can just be present and occasionally remind you of the soft gaze, the ball, and the light. Often, just knowing someone is there helps us.

Whenever you have practiced something several times and have been successful at it, you are ready for the next step. Before you move on, however, celebrate your achievements and be proud of yourself for accomplishing something that was recently very difficult for you. You should be happy and proud that you have succeeded. Successful experiences are essential to building self-confidence. Push away any doubts as to whether you will be able to do something again—they only feed your fear. I will explain more about this in a later section.

Changing Direction

We all have one side or direction that feels better for us (and for our horse) when we are riding. Always start on your safer, more comfortable side. When you've achieved a good feeling on this side through a soft gaze, the ball, the safe place, and the light, become aware of where you feel it and what it feels like. Ride in your colorful cloud of light and then change direction, taking this feeling to the new side. When you're on the new side, let your gaze soften again, let the ball sink into your pelvis, and go to your safe place and into the light that envelops you and your horse. If you lose the feeling, go back to the better side, retrieve it there, and then bring it back to the not-so-good side.

Get your good feeling back.

Scary Corners

Are you among the riders whose horse has designated certain corners as "scary"? Often, your horse once shied in this corner or at this spot, and over time, you both wind each other up at or near this location. Your expectation, your automatic assumption, is that your horse will shy in this corner. As a result, you tense up before you have even reached this spot. You might also hold your breath. This is not very pleasant for your horse, and he will also tense up. As a result, your tension increases some more, and then his does, and so forth, until the whole thing takes on a life of its own. Neither you nor your horse expects anything good from the corner because unpleasant things always happen there.

Consider this, though: does your horse shy away there only under saddle, or also on the longe or when led by hand?

If your horse shies away on the longe or when led, start by showing your horse that you no longer find the corner terrible from the ground. Apart from the fact that positive reinforcement is a good option here to remove the gremlin from the corner, it is very helpful if you manage to go into this corner in a relaxed way, and stay relaxed there.

To begin demystifying the corner, go through it without the horse and determine how you feel. Are you relaxed without the horse, or do you still have a feeling of unease? Find out how nervous this corner makes you. I had a client who got palpitations when she approached "her" corner. In such cases, it's helpful to practice first without the horse. Again, think of your safe place and the light, look softly where you are going, and think of the ball in your pelvis. If that works well, add the horse. If you don't need this first step without the horse, all the better.

If your horse also has a problem with the corner when he is led there or on the longe, be fully mindful with yourself or mentally at your safe place every time you go there. Your gaze is soft, and you are centered.

The idea is to manage to stay as calm and relaxed as possible. This will help your horse stay calm as

Objects like the camera bags here can scare your horse; remember the basics again.

well. As noted, positive reinforcement works very well, and works even better if you yourself don't get nervous.

If the problem exists only when riding, practice the same steps on your horse. You approach the corner at a walk; you are at your safe place, centered, with a soft gaze, and imagine the light in your color surrounding you. If necessary, let yourself be led through the corner initially. Successful experiences help a lot in mastering difficulties.

Faster Gaits

If you haven't trotted or cantered for a while, imagine it in self-hypnosis. Remember how it felt when it was still easy for you. Where do you feel this feeling in your body? What color is it? Take this feeling and color to your safe place; there, it becomes part of the light.

While mounted, prepare yourself with your safe place, soft gaze, sphere, and light for the next gait. Allow yourself to be put on the longe line the first few times to regain your feel for the gait. Start with a few steps or just a few moments in the faster gait, and then quickly slow down again. Initially, you should not stay in the new gait for long. Always visualize the light around you and breathe it in. Think about the sphere and "soft eyes." As the repetitions become longer and remain successful, bring these experiences into your safe place. After you've managed a few rounds without symptoms of fear, you are ready to try it without the longe line.

Continue to ride while your trusted person is with you. They can remind you of the basics. If that works well, you can also then practice alone.

Whenever you feel uncomfortable, it's likely because your gaze has turned into a fixed stare.

If you find yourself staring, let your gaze soften, and think about the sphere, your safe place, and the light. This also works while posting—and your horse will relax again when you do.

It is possible to sit centered in every gait, with a soft gaze and the idea of the ball in your pelvis. It often requires some practice to retain these ideas initially, especially when you are posting the trot, but it can be done. Always remind yourself of the basics, as the problem is often that you keep losing hold of the idea.

Jumping

Yes, you can apply everything you have read and practiced so far to jumping as well. Here, too, the rule is that you gradually work your way up to higher jumps. Start with cavalletti and get used to small hops while utilizing the basics. The more these become second nature while riding and jumping, the more confidently you can use them in higher or broader jumps, and of course in everything beyond that.

Trail Riding

When you feel you are ready to resume trail riding, you can also start leaving the grounds of the barn for ever-greater distances. Start with very short excursions, so you challenge yourself a bit but don't overwhelm yourself. You could let yourself be led or be ponied along with a lead horse, or you can also be accompanied by someone on a bicycle (if your horse is okay with bikes). Or ride a different horse for the first few attempts, if you prefer that.

Practice self-hypnosis ahead of time, and experience the ride in trance before you actually go. Always think about the basics and gradually venture further, step by step. Remember to reward yourself for your courage.

You will surely notice that your horse becomes calmer, too. A horse will immediately show that he appreciates your efforts and your work on yourself.

The basics are applicable everywhere ...

... and at every pace.

If you should experience a setback or find your fear is not gone yet, don't worry, that's not unusual.

The most common problem is that you simply forget what you should be thinking about. Therefore, it is helpful if you have a person by your side who asks you from time to time what the quality of your gaze is like or where the ball is right now, or who occasionally tells you the color of your light. After a while you won't need to be reminded of the basics anymore. Riding this way will become increasingly normal for you.

If you don't have anyone who can help you, there are other tricks you can use to keep yourself on track. Are you a rider who likes to stare at her horse's ears? Then get finger paint, or special horse-specific paint that is now available, and dab a little paint in your special color on your horse's ears, or on his mane or neck, depending on where you usually stare. You can also attach something colorful to the poll piece of his bridle. Do you always look ahead to where you are riding? As long as you are riding in the arena or indoor, you can position something in the color of your particular light at strategically convenient points to remind you of your basics. As soon as the color comes into your field of vision, raise your head, let your gaze soften, and let the ball sink into your pelvis. Imagine the light around you and breathe it in. Think of your safe place.

If you have difficulties in trance imagining that you are mastering your previous problem, such as cantering in the outdoor arena, you are allowed to become a little creative in trance. What would you need to canter there safely and calmly? Mentally go to your safe place and charge yourself with this ability through the light. If that's not enough and you need something else, how about an imaginary protective vest? If it helps, you can also supplement your imagination with a real protective vest.

Is there a past version of yourself (or a future one) who can canter wonderfully? What does this version of you wear? Special riding pants, vest, or jacket? Imagine slipping into these things, and thus into the optimal cantering situation. How does that feel?

Use what helps you in your imagination in the actual implementation as well. If you have imagined that as a secure rider, you wear a special vest, mentally slip into this vest and into this version of yourself before you get on your horse, and also actually wear this vest if you have it.

The Power of Thought

————

Hypnotherapists have long known that the neural networks of our brains can be best altered in trance. So far, no one can tell us exactly what the subconscious is, but neurobiology can at least convey approximately what happens in the subconscious brain. Nowadays, there are many studies on hypnosis and trance. For instance, a study begun in Switzerland in 2019 (contributors include the Psychiatric University Hospital Zurich, University of Zurich, ETH, Center of Dental Medicine, and OMNI) researched which regions of the brain are active in medium to deep trance. It was discovered that the pain center is subdued in trance, and that we have access to unconscious memories while in that state. Thus, we can look at the causes of problems and change the effects of these causes. Though this knowledge is invaluable, describing this approach fully is beyond the scope of this book.

Gaining access to unconscious memories with self-hypnosis alone is actually quite difficult. What we can do through self-hypnosis, however, is create new connections in our brains, or reactivate old, unused connections. By creating new connections, you will be able to react calmly instead of reacting with fear, in certain situations where fear is not beneficial and is irrational. For this to succeed, you need to feel safe. Since fear has strongly dominated your life in the past, it is first necessary to make yourself feel a feeling of safety again. You have already done this in self-hypnosis with the help of your safe place, and by recalling safe and good moments from your past. It's crucial to keep invoking this feeling because (in basic terms) this strengthens this particular neural connection. In trance, you have the best access to your feelings, which is why your neural network is best changed in that state.

You can use mental training to help strengthen specific connections by repeatedly using the ones you want to reinforce, even in a conscious-awake state. It also makes sense to weaken the old fear connection at the same time. This is possible by combining two techniques, and I will explain how this works in the next section.

TECHNIQUES FOR THOUGHT CONTROL

You already know that you reinforce your fear when you continuously focus on it and think about what scares you. Thus, it's important to control your thoughts, because your thoughts influence your feelings and your behavior. A very well-known technique to control your thoughts is thought-stopping, which goes like this: Every time you have a thought related to your fear—for example, "Oh, it's very windy today, my horse will be very nervous. Maybe I should not ride"—you say to yourself, "Stop!" and imagine a stop sign in your mind. Every time your thoughts go in this direction, repeat the exercise. If you feel that this technique helps you, keep using it.

An alternative method is thought diversion, which works even better for a lot of people. Instead of stopping your thoughts, you divert them towards more pleasant or productive subjects, which decreases the stress level in your body at the same time. For example, in the scenario described above, you could divert your thoughts to your safe place and your light.

Every time you notice you are mentally dealing with your fear, let your gaze soften and let the ball drop into your pelvis. To divert your thoughts, briefly visit your safe place in your mind and imagine the light around you. Take a breath from that light. Imagine that you are inhaling the color of the light deeply. The light gives you protection and safety and contains everything you need for your well-being.

Creating and Strengthening New Connections

You have already learned that you can best create neural connections in trance by imagining something with intense focus. Each time you do this, you strengthen the existing connection. It is not important how you use this connection—whether you use it in trance or in a conscious-awake state, mentally or in real-life experience. The only difference is the intensity with which the connection is strengthened through your imagination.

Of course, you don't get full benefits from just riding in your imagination. Your brain doesn't care whether you're just imagining something or if it's actually happening, but muscle cells also have a memory, in a manner of speaking. Therefore, you will need to test yourself while riding in order to create new, positive muscle memory.

Don't worry, you don't have to jump a 1.20m oxer if you haven't jumped for years. Our goal is to strengthen your successful experiences related to your new connections, not to overwhelm you (which would only reactivate the wrong connections). Without the physical experience of riding, however, you won't be able to face what has scared you so far. As before, a systematic approach will help you with this.

Only when you succeed in trance, and you can also vividly imagine it while awake, can you make it a reality while riding. Meanwhile, continue to work with self-hypnosis. This process is best explained with an example.

Anne last went trail riding three years ago. During this ride, her horse bolted, and although nothing happened to Anne, trail riding became impossible for her. Since then, the carefree feeling she used to have while riding, even inside, has disappeared. More and more often, fear rode along with her, although in the arena, at least, Anne managed to ignore the fear and ride anyway. Anne has done a lot of self-hypnosis lately. She has a safe place that works well for her, and she often thinks about it during the day. She has noticed that riding is increasingly bringing her joy again, and she wishes to go trail riding very soon. Instead of just trying to hit the trails right away, however, she is taking a gradual approach.

Anne has already created her future in self-hypnosis and experienced herself riding off-premises in trance. During trance, she felt how she rode her horse. Her horse felt loose and relaxed, and Anne felt free. She felt freedom in her belly, which was completely relaxed and joyful, and she felt the connection to her horse in her heart. It was a totally beautiful feeling, and she absorbed it, breathed it in, and took it to her safe place, where it became part of the light.

In her safe place, she also placed a framed picture of this ride. This picture shows her and her horse cantering on a forest path. Anne beams with happiness, her cheeks aglow and slightly reddened by the wind. Sunlight falls through the foliage, creating dappled points of light on the sandy ground. Whenever Anne is in trance in her safe place, she looks at the picture and absorbs the feeling she has during this imagined ride.

Since she now wants to make such a trail ride a reality, she makes a rough plan. She will first go with a rider and friend who will pony Anne's horse, though Anne will also take the reins. She doesn't want to risk proceeding too fast, so she came up with this idea of giving some of the control to her friend. In trance, she has now imagined this situation, allowing herself to feel it. Also, while awake, she has thought about this plan and can imagine it well—she has a good feeling about it. Anne and her friend successfully do a short trail ride at a walk, and afterward Anne is very proud of herself. Over the next days and weeks, she goes a step further every time, and after a while, a brisk canter on the forest path is also possible. She feels completely safe, and also feels confident because she knows what she could do if she should by some chance get nervous.

What we can learn from this process is that only when something feels good in your thoughts does it make sense for you to make it a reality. This way, we create successful outcomes and avoid setbacks. It is very important that you face your challenges step by step, without overwhelming yourself.

Safety First

Riding is not a risk-free sport, which you surely know. However, most accidents involving horses happen while handling, not riding. This is because, over time, we tend to let our guard down. We often forget that a horse is a flight animal, and we gradually overlook the precautionary behaviors that were initially drilled into us.

Always be attentive when dealing with your horse. Stay alert and in the moment, and stay off your phone. Anyone who leads or rides their horse while using their phone often misses what's happening around them. This leads to slower reactions, and is simply not safe.

Beyond awareness, there is a reason why close-toed boots or ankle boots, gloves, and a helmet are part of safe riding gear. It makes sense to use them. Moreover, it is advisable to ride with a safety vest, especially if it makes you feel better.

Take advantage of anything you can use to make you feel safe and confident, including appropriate riding apparel. Your goal is not to eventually ride without protective gear, of course, but to fully enjoy riding again. Maintaining your equipment is therefore also part of increasing your safety and ultimately your enjoyment. Taking care to clean and treat leather and other materials on a regular basis can extend their lifespan, but tack won't last forever. So make it a practice to schedule regular inspections of your equipment and keep it in good condition.

In addition to making sure your gear is in good shape, it's a good idea to make sure you can be located, especially when you go trail riding. It's always safer to ride out with someone else, I don't need to tell you that, but if you want to ride alone, there are simple measures you can take in case something happens.

For example, these days there are good apps available for your phone so you can be found, or so you can find your way back if you get lost. Having your phone with you also means you can call for help if you need it. Such precautions can give you increased peace of mind and tranquility, because you know you are prepared. You don't have to fear that you are not safe.

All of this doesn't mean, of course, that you will always have everything under control. That would be too much to ask; some things in life simply can't be controlled. Therefore, if you ever feel you are dealing with too much, be willing to seek help.

Still Worried?

Setbacks are no reason to think your strategy isn't working. They are part of the process and are not always avoidable—though this doesn't mean that you should automatically expect them, either. Setbacks can occur as long as the neural connections underlying your fear still exist and are not entirely dismantled. Setbacks also often occur when we are going through a challenging time.

A client of mine who had panic attacks along with fear discovered under hypnosis that the unprocessed death of her father during her childhood was the cause of her fear. Once she recognized this, things improved. However, a few months later she suddenly started experiencing fears again, though not as severely as before. I believed that something must have triggered the resurgence of her fear, so we talked it through. Over the phone, we figured out that her renewed fear was linked to a death in her circle of friends. Knowing that, she intensified her self-hypnosis, and the fear went away again. It's been several years now since her last fear episode, and she has been basically fear-free ever since.

Relapses often occur due to the following reasons:

- **Something similar to whatever originally caused the fear happens again. Often, as in the case of my client, these are significant life events.**

- **Something else dramatic happens that completely throws you off track. Even if this event has nothing to do with the original cause of your fear, it ensures that your life is generally turned upside down. Examples of this are severe illnesses, deaths, separations, bullying, or other trauma.**

- **You stop the self-hypnosis and exercises too early. You think everything is going well, so you stop the exercises, skip the self-hypnosis, and don't restart them even when you notice the fear is gradually returning.**

If you notice your fear is creeping back, there's no reason why you should let it take hold again. You can turn things around. If you've already managed to ride relatively fear-free, it will be much easier this time to let go of the fear entirely. All you need in order to achieve this is a little more commitment.

Redirect Your Thoughts

The most important thing to do when you realize you are thinking about your fears is to immediately redirect your thoughts. The more we engage with our fears, the stronger they become. This must be very clear to you by now. Even if you are free of fear most of the time, it is possible to reactivate that fear if you allow yourself to doubt and wonder whether the fear will come back.

Whenever you notice you are doubting yourself or thinking about your fear, redirect your thoughts: soften your gaze, let the ball drop into your pelvis, mentally go to your safe place, and imagine the light around you that gives you protection and safety. Breathe it in deeply and imagine it filling you up. Afterwards, engage in something else to

Better safe than sorry! Never ride without a properly fitted helmet.

distract yourself from your negative thoughts as much as possible.

Tips and Tricks

Sometimes, unfortunately, it is our fellow human beings who cause us to start doubting whether something is effective. Some people always have to give their two cents and are very pessimistic in their views, which sabotages your progress. So, when in doubt, be careful who you talk to about working on your fear. You are suggestible, meaning you are very receptive to things people tell you, especially when the topic has a high emotional impact for you. Don't let anyone tarnish your efforts or doubt your successes.

I have experienced this myself quite often. A few years ago, when I was sick with myocarditis (inflammation of the heart muscle), things were not looking good. In times like that, many things get put into perspective, and you adopt a different outlook. Such an illness makes you acutely aware of your mortality—mainly because, in my case, the doctors did not dare make a prognosis. They made it very clear that I probably would not recover and that I should get my affairs in order in case I didn't survive.

My physicians and acquaintances had made me aware of the potential consequences of myocarditis, and, of course, were also conscious of the fact that I might not survive this disease. However, I simply didn't believe in the possibility of not recovering. I was sure I would live, work, and, naturally, ride again. I clarified what should happen in case I didn't make it, but otherwise, I didn't allow myself to think about it. I trained myself to not think about it, in fact, so I wouldn't become overwhelmed by negative, fearful possibilities.

What was hard for me to endure were comments from other people. One day, I went to the barn, which I made a point of doing once every week. This weekly visit to my horse was the absolute highlight of my life at this point. Every Saturday, I was driven to the barn, gave Gitano an apple, and petted him a bit. Then I had to sit down. Afterward, I was taken back home. Most of my barn visit was spent sitting, and sadly, I was so exhausted after 15 to 20 minutes that we had to leave.

I know it is hard for those who see me now to imagine how it was for me back then.

On one of these visits, I was leaning against Gitano, who was happily crunching his apple, when a fellow boarder asked me how I was doing. "I'm improving," I said.

She said, "Hmm, it doesn't look like it. I had an acquaintance with myocarditis. He is now six feet under." And with these words, she left the barn.

I often wonder why people behave this way, and destroy someone else's hope. They probably are not aware of the damage they are causing. However, this isn't a good excuse, and we should all become much more aware of the power of our words. It seems to me that people sometimes do this just to join in a conversation, to revel in gossip. And what is the most "fun" to gossip about? Horror stories. Every mother has a tale about being told horrifying birth stories while heavily pregnant. It is no wonder that these stories can have negative effects.

That fellow boarder was not the only one who told me stories of people who had died of myocarditis. But I didn't let it get to me. Fortunately, even back then, I was already well-versed in self-hypnosis and could protect myself from these kinds of negative suggestions, and as I mentioned above, I trained myself to not think about it.

You can respond in the same way. If someone tries to bring back your fear, out of concern or some other motive, protect yourself from it and mentally engage in something else. Imagine the light around you that repels everything negative. In such a situation, you can also perform Pika-Pika breathing (see page 78) or conduct a mindfulness exercise. Mindfulness exercises can also be used very well as thought-interrupters when you notice you are dealing with doubts or fears.

PROBLEMS AND SOLUTIONS

You will likely realize how often your thoughts are consumed by fears and doubts only when you start paying attention to them. You might feel somewhat overwhelmed by this. You might then get the idea that you are at the mercy of your thoughts and can't control them. However, this is not true. You can change your thoughts, even if it doesn't come naturally and you have to work for it. Practice makes perfect in this case, too.

If your thought control worked well to start with, but suddenly you are having problems with it, change your strategy. If you have always worked with a soft gaze and the ball, try Pika-Pika breathing instead, or see how it goes with mindfulness exercises. The next time you start thinking about your fear, look around the room and find five things you see, five sounds you hear, five sensations at the surface of your body; then find four of each, then three, then two, and then one. If you do this very consciously, your thoughts about fear should have become secondary. Afterward, it's best to engage in something different that requires your full attention.

You can also listen to the MP3 "Mastering Situations" on a daily basis, practice self-hypnosis regularly, or both. For the next while, focus on steps 2 to 5 in your itinerary, which is explained in the following section.

What Now? Your Roadmap for the Future

You might be feeling a bit overwhelmed by the abundance of information and tasks you now have after reading this book. But don't worry. As they say, Rome wasn't built in a day, and you don't have to implement everything immediately or all at once. Remember Beppo, the streetsweeper from the book *Momo*? He had a seemingly endless street to sweep, but he didn't think about its entire length. He focused on each step and movement of his broom, and made his task manageable. This seemingly small shift in perspective has a huge impact, and I recommend that you keep Beppo in mind as an example for your own journey.

Put one foot in front of the other, and stay focused on what you are doing. If you find it easy, add another task. After you have worked with self-hypnosis and the other exercises for some time, use the scale of 1 to 10 to assess how your fear has changed. Do you remember the note where you evaluated your fear and its symptoms? Look at it now and then to check your progress. You should do this at most every 14 days. Between these checks, your horse will show you how well you are managing to diminish your fear.

No worries, you will also be able to relax on your horse.

Your Itinerary

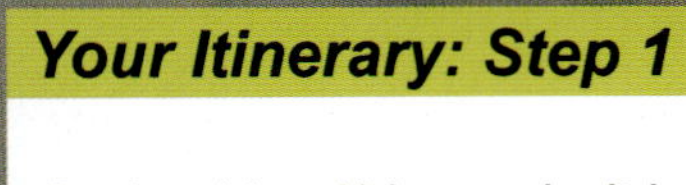

Your Itinerary: Step 1

Begin with self-hypnosis. It is important that you find your safe place. Also, repeatedly think about this place during the day and imagine the light around you. Put something that is the color of the light in your safe place in a spot you often see, and practice your soft gaze and the ball whenever the object catches your attention. Think about your safe place and the light, especially whenever you think about your fear or start to doubt yourself. And, of course, immerse yourself in your safe place when you go to your horse—before mounting, repeatedly while riding, and after you dismount. You should practice this daily for the first few weeks. Also, listen to the MP3 "Mastering Situations" as often as possible.

Most readers will probably only need this first step to achieve success. If you are unsure or have a relapse, though, continue with the other steps.

Your Itinerary: Step 2

In trance, go from your safe place to a secure moment in your past, and to a moment when you successfully accomplished something. Take these feelings back to your safe place. There, they become part of the light.

Your Itinerary: Step 3

In this step, do a blockage resolution in self-hypnosis. Perform this only once, specifically when you feel you have found a good safe place. After that, go back to Step 1.

Your Itinerary: Step 4

Create a future vision in trance from your safe place. Take the feelings from it back to your safe place, and let them become part of the light. Go back to Step 1.

Your Itinerary: Step 5

Go into self-hypnosis daily and work with positive suggestions, as well as repeatedly listening to the MP3 "Mastering Situations." Put something that is the color of the light from your safe place in a spot you often see, and practice your soft gaze and the ball whenever the object catches your eye. Then always think about your safe place and the light. Do this whenever you think about your fear or have doubts. And, of course, immerse yourself in your safe place when you go to your horse—before mounting, repeatedly while riding, and after dismounting.

If everything is working well so far, you can gradually begin to listen to the MP3 less often, or do self-hypnosis less often. Always mentally return to your safe place if you become insecure while riding. Your soft gaze and the ball are exercises you should implement for the rest of your equestrian life.

Conclusion

In this book, I have provided you with a lot of information. Now it's up to you to find out what works best when you need to redirect your thoughts, and to regularly practice self-hypnosis. I hope the audio files and video sequences help you implement what you've learned.

I've tried to include many of the problems I've encountered in my work so far, and to provide numerous examples. It's possible that I might not have addressed your specific issue, though; if that's the case, consider joining the Facebook group for this book, titled "Equihypnosis—get over riding fear." There, I answer questions in live videos, and you can interact with other readers. Alternatively, feel free to email me at **nicole@performabilityllc.com**. I will do my best to assist you in writing if possible. You are also welcome to reach out if you want to organize a clinic or work with me in person, one-on-one.

I would be especially thrilled to hear about your successes. Please write to me about your experiences on your journey.

You have my wholehearted wish for success on your continued fearless path, and endless joy with your horse.

With all my love,

Nicole Weber

How to reach Nicole:
nicole@performabilityllc.com
www.equihypnosis.com

Selected Bibliography

Czarnecki, Sylvia. *Ehrlich motiviert!: Positives Training mit Pferden*. Cadmos, 2017.

Dunning, Angela. *The Horse Leads the Way: Honoring the True Role of the Horse in Equine   Facilitated Practice*. YouCaxton Publications, 2017.

Ende, Michael. *Momo*. Piper, 2009.

Freud, Sigmund. *The Collected Works of Sigmund Freud*. PergamonMedia, 2015..

Hallberg, Leif. *The Clinical Practice of Equine-Assisted Therapy: Including Horses In Human Healthcare*. Routledge, 2018.

McCormick, Adele von Rüst, and Marlena Deborah McCormick. *Horse Sense and the Human Heart: What Horses Can Teach Us About Trust, Bonding, Creativity and Spirituality*. Health Communications, Inc., 1997.

Roth, Gerhard and Nicole Strüber. *Wie das Gehirn die Seele macht*. Klett-Cotta, 2014.

Shambo, Leigh, David Young and Catherine Madera. *The Listening Heart: The Limbic Path Beyond Office Therapy*. Human-Equine Alliances for Learning (HEAL), 2013.

Swift, Sally. *Centered Riding*. Trafalgar Square Books, 1985.

Swift, Sally. *Centered Riding 2: Further Exploration*. Trafalgar Square Books, 2014.

Waldo, Andrea Monsarrat. *Brain Training for Riders: Unlock Your Riding Potential with Stressless Techniques for Conquering Fear, Improving Performance, and Finding Focused Calm*. Trafalgar Square Books, 2016.

Acknowledgments

This book would never have been created without the support of many people. I would like to thank Ute Flockenhaus for the great seminar and your valuable help with writing. Many thanks to Stéphane Etrillard, tireless mentor, intellectual, and lateral thinker, for your faith in my projects; thanks also for everything I have learned and am still able to learn from you—and of course for your constant encouragement to write.

Many thanks to Bettina Baldin, friend, trainer, and world's best photo model. You have been with me and my horses for years, and I am grateful to you for so many things! I would like to thank Michelle Schlicker for the beautiful photos. Many thanks also to Angelika Engberg for your insightful introduction to the world of Centered Riding: every seminar with you opens my eyes further. Dear Jenny, dear Peer, I am glad that we got to know each other, and I am grateful for your contributions to this project.

I would like to thank Claudia Weingand for her feedback after reading the first draft of this book—it would not have existed without you, either. Sincere thanks also go to Claudia König and the entire Müller Rüschlikon team, who first published this book in German. I appreciate all of the supportive phone calls, chatter, and important information. To the entire team at Trafalgar Square Books, especially Rebecca, Lizzie and Martha: Thanks for believing in my manuscript. Thank you for bringing my book into the world!

The support of my family has been, and continues to be, so very meaningful. I am grateful to have grown up in an environment where books are important and there are role models who live according to their own values. I am also grateful to my many clients and their horses for allowing me to accompany them on their journeys to free themselves from fear. Without you, I would have had nothing to write.

I would like to thank all the four-legged companions who have repeatedly guided me back to my path. Jamesy James, world's best dog soul, you have opened my eyes to many things, and the memory of you was very much alive while I was writing. Schnuppi and Hase, the doggo, and the kitties, have also made their contributions. For my own journey, I especially thank Gitano, my PRE-Lusitano cross, to whom I owe my life and the health of my heart. I wish for many more happy years with this horse soul, who came to me as a bit of a rogue and who now enriches my life with his fine mind. Gitano, you have been my co-therapist for years, and you always show me exactly when something is wrong.

Most of all, I thank Maren. You believe in me, always have my back, and make sure I don't starve. I couldn't wish for anyone better by my side, to faithfully and lovingly accompany me on all my adventures. Ultimately, this book is for you. I will not give up hope that one day we will hit the trails together.